D1707644

JILL McDOWELL

Lost in Mother Russia

A MEMOIR

ISBN (print): 978-1-54399-593-0

ISBN (eBook): 978-1-54399-594-7

Publishers note: Some characters and events in this memoir are fictitious. Any similarity to real persons, living or dead, is coincidental and not intended by the author.

Printed and bound in the United States of America

Email: writerjill.5@gmail.com

TABLE OF CONTENTS

AUTHOR'S NOTE

Probably just jetlag, I reassured myself, having returned only the day before from my eleventh trip to Russia. Although not nearly as loud as the Aeroflot jumbo jet engines accompanying me on my flight from Moscow to Los Angeles, but every bit as persistent, the annoying voice now droned on as I tried to peruse *The LA Times*, spread out in front of me on my dining room table. The combined on-ground and in-air travel time from Moscow's Sheremetovo Airport to Los Angeles International had been twenty-seven hours. Yes, jetlag was an entirely plausible explanation for the noise which was reminiscent of a buzzing mosquito circling my bed in search of its midnight snack. As it became more insistent, the nagging voice became more recognizable; it appeared to be American, with a cadence similar to my own, and I thought I also detected a touch of Canadian, with just a hint of Slavic. Yes, most certainly related to jetlag. (I hoped.)

"Tell your story, tell your story," reiterated the articulate nag. "You have, after all, just returned from two adventuresome years in Russia, the land of your ancestors." Well, only infrequently do I pay heed to auditory hallucinations arising from jetlagged exhaustion, but the nagging little voice wouldn't shut up. Alright, already—Not only will I tell my story; I'll write it as well. And, dear reader, here it is.

> *Schastliviye puteshestviya!*
> Happy travels!
> Jill McDowell
> Lacey, Washington
> 2/2/2020

ABOUT THE AUTHOR

Jill McDowell was born in Canada, spent fifty years in Southern California and—hoping to see rain once more before she dies—has now settled in the Pacific Northwest. The weather has not disappointed.

When not applying pen to paper or fingers to keyboard, she enjoys classical music. Mozart—whose beautifully maintained piano she saw and admired in Prague—remains her favorite composer.

A degree in Drama from Occidental College, theater has likewise played a role in her life. During her freshman year at the University of Washington she performed on stage at the Showboat Theater; toured with a Shakespearean production directed by Duncan Ross, a noteworthy figure with the Bristol Old Vic Theatre School; and worked as an on-camera announcer at the local Seattle PBS channel.

More recently, in her role as a grandmother presenting a plateful of chocolate chip cookies to megastar Drake—part of a skit the pair performed prior to a nationally telecast NBA Awards show—Ms. McDowell, at the pinnacle of fame, chose to give up her barely established career as a commercial actor. She likewise ended her partially successful attempt at becoming the oldest living voiceover actor in Southern California where she voiced a forty-five-year-old elephant—typecasting at its best.

During her half century in the workforce, the author toiled as a publicity director at a San Francisco TV station; a medical transcriptionist for physicians whose speech was often more difficult to decode than their handwriting; a government employee; and as a starving artist with Peaceable Beasts, her own art-rubber-stamp company. She spent two years (1995-1996) teaching English at Moscow State University as well as at the Japanese Embassy School in Moscow, thereby affording her a tri-cultural experience. Armed with a 100-year-old map and the exceptional navigational skills of a personable driver, she found her way to Norka, the tiny Russian village where her ancestors lived from 1763 to 1900.

She taught English as a Second Language (ESL) for thirty-five years, and recently retired from Glendale Community College in Southern California, where she was an assistant adjunct ESL professor.

In addition to the Czech Republic and Russia, she has also travelled to Poland, Lithuania, Estonia and Belarus; Finland, France, Germany, Italy, and England; and to most of the provinces in Canada.

ACKNOWLEDGEMENTS

Many thanks to the members of my critique group—Karen Bishop, Barbara M. Crawford, Dave Gardner and Steve Adams. I am grateful for their ongoing support; for their encouragement and suggestions; for reading, re-reading and helping to edit my manuscript. And, I am especially grateful for their sense of humor, as well as for their appreciation of mine. Kudos to all who spent many hours developing, coordinating and expanding our Writers Read oral presentations, and a special nod to Dave who came up with the idea in the first place. Thank you for inviting me to read from *Lost in Mother Russia* at several of these events; I enjoyed myself immensely, particularly since the excerpts and I were both very well received. Who says writing need be a solitary endeavor?

A nod of appreciation to my friend Nancy McIntyre for her witticisms, a couple of which have found their way into episode titles for this memoir. And for Li, with love, as always.

Oh, and of course to my cat, Muffin, who brings surprise into my life daily as she attempts to knock the framed artwork off the walls; dismay as she systematically removes all contents from the pigeonholes in my well-scratched desk; aggravation in her decisive (although—in my estimation—unnecessary) edits of my manuscript; and a heightened sense of anticipation in never knowing what to expect next. Oh, oh! Got to go—Muffin's at work editing again!

Syevo Khoroshova!
All the best!

Episode One

JOBLESS IN MOSCOW

I had finally found work in Russia! That it began in winter only added to the excitement. My job was to teach English at Polyglot Language Institute in Moscow, a private school owned and operated by a young Turkish-American woman. Jenna arranged for my work visa, found a two-room shared apartment for me, told me to dress warmly, and said she'd meet me at Sheremetovo Airport in Moscow.

Although I was born in Canada during fifty below zero weather, I grew up in Southern California. Except for a few skiing trips, my experience with true winter weather was limited before my arrival in Moscow on January 6, 1995.

I should also mention that I am extremely directionally challenged. However, during my first few freezing days in Moscow, I worked out a very good plan to orient myself by utilizing snowbanks as landmarks. What a great idea! It worked really well! That is, until on the third day my snowdrifts seemed to have relocated themselves.

As I say, I'm profoundly directionally challenged, so I assumed **I** was the one who had relocated. It took a few more days for me to realize that my snowy landmarks were being pushed here and there by the equivalent of Muscovite Zambonis. Sometimes I really wish I weren't map-dyslexic.

There was another challenge living in Moscow in winter. Angelinos worry about earthquakes, Santa Ana winds, brush fires, too much or too little rain, traffic congestion, but definitely not about icicles. In 1995 icicles were pretty low on my list of stressors. One particularly slushy afternoon I noted several workers perched atop the building I was about to enter. They all had picks or shovels in hand, and they shouted something to me from the rooftop.

Not wanting to reveal my less than perfect Russian, I waved and said, "*Spasibo*—thank you." Probably telling me to have a nice day I thought.

In retrospect it was more likely: "*Zhenshena!* Hey lady—Ya wanna get impaled by an icicle? *Bozhe moy! Shto eto takoy?!*"

I worked at Polyglot Language Institute for about three months, until I was called in by the assistant director, Brian, a British expat. He had bad news for me—the students wanted a younger teacher.

"No, actually they don't," I said.

The students were, for the most part, beautiful young Russian women of marriageable age. They didn't necessarily want a younger teacher—they just wanted a single **male** teacher of any age who was still breathing. Most of my students dreamed of marrying an American and relocating to the US. I didn't meet those qualifications and was therefore let go.

It didn't help either that Polyglot had recently posted on their office walls a quotation from Britain's Prince Charles, saying: "American English is such a substandard language that it should not be allowed to be taught anywhere but in America." Not only did my students want to get married, they wanted to speak the English of Shakespeare. Time to find another job!

I combed the expatriate English-language newspaper for job ads. I went to the American and Canadian Embassies to see if they needed any workers. They didn't. Did they have any leads? They didn't. Finally, a promising ad appeared in the local newspaper. Moscow State University—one of Russia's leading institutions of higher learning—needed someone to teach English to graduate students.

I applied, interviewed, and got the job. I had taught English before at private schools in Southern California, but had absolutely no experience teaching university students. I was hired in the springtime of 1995, but wouldn't begin teaching at the University until August. I was so anxious that I spent much of the spring and summer fantasizing about getting hit by a Moscow bus so that I wouldn't have to face a group of eager PhD students, all of whom had far more education than I. I'm happy to report that no bus collided with me, and I remained at *Moskovskiy gosydarstveniy universitet*—MGU—for two full memorable years.

During my search for a new job after Polyglot had sacked me, I also spotted a notice on the bulletin board at the American Embassy. It seemed the Japanese Embassy in Moscow was looking for an English teacher—specifically one who spoke American English. Take that Prince Charles!

After a week or two of trilingual communications, the Japanese Embassy sent a chauffeur to pick me up and take me to head-quarters for my interview. The Japanese school was located on the upper floors of the French Embassy School, situated in a wooded area just off a major Moscow boulevard. My escorts and I tramped up seven flights of stairs in our winter boots until we arrived at a wall lined with cubicles. I was to remove my boots, store them in my own cubicle, and put on a pair of slippers reserved for guests.

The interview was conducted in English, Russian and Japanese. I spoke English and less than perfect Russian; the Japanese spoke Japanese, fractured English and fractured Russian, and our interpreter, Nikolai, spoke all three languages fluently. The Japanese had a very difficult time with my name, Jill McDowell, as the sound of the letter "l" does not exist in Japanese. The closest they could come to approximating my name was Jiroo McDowroo. We finally decided they could call me by my first name and tack an honorific title on the end; hence I became Jiroo-sen-say.

During my two-hour interview I periodically glanced at my slippered feet. Oh my God! Had I forgotten to put on my shoes that morning? Was I, even more shockingly, still attired in my bathrobe? No, fortunately I was appropriately dressed, but I would need quite some time to get used to being interviewed in slippers.

It took about a month for the Japanese Embassy to do my background check and approve my credentials. Representatives called repeatedly to confirm my age—apparently, they wanted someone older rather than younger. But then, their K-thru-12 students weren't planning on getting married to an American anytime soon. Now I had two jobs! I could remain in Russia at least a full year, until the expiration of my work permit.

Polyglot still owed me money since laying me off, so I paid them a visit. I hadn't planned to say a thing to them about my dual successes at finding work. I met with Brian the Brit who asked me how I was doing. He obviously didn't see much hope for my job prospects as a middle-aged woman, and he attempted to commiserate, somewhat insincerely it seemed to me.

"Well," I said. "Moscow State University has hired me to teach English in their graduate business program."

"What, you got that job?" a flummoxed Brian responded.

"Yes, and I was even luckier. Not only will I be teaching at MGU, but I've also been hired by the Japanese Embassy as well."

"You mean you got that job, too!?"

TAKE THAT BRIAN—YOU BRIT! Apparently, Brian had also applied for both jobs, but I, despite my advancing age and American accent, had come out the victor!

Episode Two

KEEPING MY COOL AT THIRTY-NINE-BELOW!

In addition to teaching six English conversation classes a week at the Japanese Embassy School in Moscow, I was unofficially appointed the cultural liaison there. Often, I encouraged my Japanese colleagues, Junko and Noriko, to accompany me and my Russian friends on outings. Junko had a sporty red Toyota with a control panel plastered with knobs, or, as my Russian friend and landlady, Nadya, enjoyed calling them, "kanobichkis".

One lovely summer day we three middle aged ladies—Junko, Noriko and I—set out for the countryside. It was a beautiful drive through Mother Russia. We stopped periodically to purchase blueberries, raspberries, honey, radishes, dill, cucumbers, tomatoes, potatoes, and pots and pans from the roadside vendors. We weren't at all tempted by the beach towels decorated with the Beatles, scantily clad pin-up girls, or the American flag.

Junko, who was driving, had a much better sense of direction than I, but we still needed to stop for directions once along the way. We pulled into a rutted field on a remote countryside farm, two Japanese ladies in the front seat of the little red Toyota and one American in the back. Junko and Noriko spoke minimal English and slightly more Russian; I spoke less than perfect Russian and no Japanese. I was assigned the role of interpreter whenever we interacted with the locals.

A babushka came out of her farmhouse, greeted us, and gazed in amazement at the sight before her. I'm sure it was the first time she had encountered such a trio of foreigners seemingly speaking not a single language fluently. We complimented her on her vegetable garden and exchanged pleasantries as best as our language skills permitted. She gave us directions; we thanked her profusely, and were on our way again. No doubt the babushka and her friends chuckled for quite some time about the encounter with the little red Toyota and the Babel of languages emanating from within.

On another occasion, Christmas Eve, 1995, Noriko and I set out for Suzdal. Suzdal is an exquisitely beautiful one-thousand-year-old village along the Golden Ring of Russia. *Zolotoya kaltzso*, or the Golden Ring, is made up of eight more equally exquisite ancient towns which grew to encircle Moscow from the Middle Ages to the present.

It was cold—thirty-nine degrees below zero! It was *very* cold!! Noriko and I were travelling with a group of forty or so tourists aboard a Mercedes Benz bus. The tour guide claimed the heater had only recently broken, but I think it more likely the bus never had a heater. Among our group were two couples from Florida. They, like me, had purchased a full assortment of winter clothing from

L.L. Bean and Eddie Bauer, including four pairs of khaki-green, tractor-tread knee-high insulated boots. These were not very stylish, but they were warm.

A man from the Netherlands, on the other hand (or feet) sported lightweight loafers. "But when it snows in Holland, it's never this cold; how was I to know?" Similarly, a baldheaded German was fretting because he had forgotten to bring his winter hat; when frostbite threatened his scalp, he got back on the unheated bus. And his seatmate, a Frenchwoman, was wearing high-heeled unlined boots; her shivering body and chattering teeth somewhat marred her otherwise elegant style. It seemed the only non-Russians who really took winter weather seriously were those of us from the warmest areas, four Floridians and one Californian.

I was dressed in long underwear, ski pants, a turtleneck, a Russian floral scarf, a fleece jacket, a full length down coat, knee socks, legwarmers, warm winter boots, and heavy wool mittens. Noriko had forgotten her mittens. Now, I understand how you might forget your sunglasses or your lipstick, but I'll never understand how you can forget your mittens in thirty-nine-below-zero weather. Even **with** my mittens I was still freezing, and the balaclava I had over my head and face wasn't helping much. I wasn't wearing earrings, though, as I had been warned that they were likely to freeze to my ears.

It was so cold on our five-hour journey that all but one of the rest stops were cancelled. On previous excursions, the bathroom had generally consisted of a grove of trees by the side of the road; men on one side and ladies on the other. But barren winter trees provided only minimal privacy. And there was also the danger of freezing our backsides off.

Truth be told, a grove of trees, whatever the season, was generally preferable to an actual public toilet, which, it would seem, had not been cleaned since the Khrushchev era. That is, if you could actually find a public toilet. And, FYI, depending on your needs, it's wise to specify a toilet, unless, of course, you plan to take a bath.

Moscow, in 1995, had only two known public toilets. Known, that is, to my circle of Japanese, Canadian, Finnish, British, American, French, and Russian friends. Well, yes, that does exclude facilities found in the Bolshoi Theatre, museums, concert halls, and other sites requiring ticketed admission. But, still, that's in a city of over twelve million people.

Hence, when McDonald's Golden Arches (not to be confused with the Golden Ring mentioned earlier) sprang up not far from Red Square, availability of public facilities increased by thirty-three percent. Yes, one **was** expected to purchase a "gamburger", but that, I think, was a small price to pay to use the cleanest toilet in the biggest city of the world's largest country.

But I digress. Back to the Golden Ring. Brisk winter weather notwithstanding, Christmas in Suzdal was magical, highlighted as it was by a festive dinner, tea from a wood-fired samovar, and caroling at midnight. Next morning, for those hardy enough to brave the cold—and that included me and my Japanese colleague, Junko—we were treated to a ride round the village in a troika.

Reminiscent of the writings of Chekhov or Tolstoy, a trio (or troika) of horses had already been harnessed to a well-worn wooden sleigh. The horse and sleigh (also collectively called a troika) were standing ready to transport us over the sparkling icy roadway. Our driver, also evocative of a character from Russian literature, wore his traditional hat with earflaps (*schlapa*), but he apparently saw no need to pull the flaps down over his ears.

He wore no gloves or mittens, and his large calloused hands were red and raw. His feet, however, were protected in a pair of *valyenki*, the boiled felt boots favored by peasants of yore and country folks of today. And, after putting on thick scratchy wool socks that morning, for added warmth, he had, more than likely, wrapped his legs with pages from *Pravda*, the official State newspaper. Yes, this practical communist journal had yet another purpose besides substituting for fish wrap and toilet paper!

Yoked three abreast (in customary troika fashion), and sporting colorful thick blankets, the horses seemed to enjoy the nippy minus-forty-degree weather. My camera, on the other hand, did not. Alas, I have no photos from Christmas in Suzdal, as the shutter mechanism on my Canon "press-here-dummy" camera had frozen solid.

Junko and I crunched our way through freshly fallen snow. Our driver, Sasha, helped us navigate icy patches on the narrow roadway, and then settled the two of us into the sleigh. He covered our legs with blankets three inches deep which bore a striking resemblance to those worn by the horses. Although their muzzles were covered in frost, the horses appeared warmer than their passengers. And Sasha, with a frosty moustache rather than a muzzle, seemed to be the warmest of all. The horses were decked out with large colorful bells wreathed around their necks and fastened to their harnesses as well. These bells jangled festively when our driver signaled the equine trio to speed up from a trot to a canter and then briefly into a daredevil gallop. Four-wheel drive was not needed here.

While completing our final lap around Suzdal, we suddenly swerved to avoid a rut in our path. The metal runners on our sleigh scraped and skidded across the ice as we careened towards a snowbank. The experienced horses were up to the slippery challenge, and after steadying themselves, they gave what sounded like a collective self-congratulatory snort. The horse at the center of the trio whinnied for good measure.

Our quintessentially Russian tour was about to end. Our coachman gently reined in his horses, and, somewhat like shifting gears on a car, guided his three animals from a slow trot to a walk, and then finally eased them to a halt. After giving a sugar cube to each of his beasts, Sasha unblanketed Junko and me. He helped us out of the sleigh and wished us well—*syevo khoroshova*. He didn't wish us a Merry Christmas, however, as it was the twenty-fifth of December and Russian Orthodox Christmas wouldn't arrive until January sixth.

Episode Three
ESPIONAGE REROUTED

It might come as something of a surprise that one of my adventures at the Japanese Embassy School in Moscow involved a piranha. My new colleague, Hiroshi Sato, had recently been sent from Japan to teach English grammar at the school. Apparently, Mr. Sato liked fish, the more exotic the better. He thought it would be educational for his students to have a pet fish with an overbite. He hadn't counted on dropping the fish bowl along with the cannibal fish on the first day of class. The glass shattered and the fish flopped onto the floor. Hiroshi managed to protect his students as well as saving the piranha. He wasn't bitten, but he cut his hand badly on the broken glass and needed to have treatment at the local clinic. No one ever saw the fish again after that, and it was rumored that Hiroshi Sato had eaten the piranha as sushi.

Almost every Friday night at the Canadian Embassy I attended informal gatherings for Canuck expats. Occasionally, as a US citizen, I had official dealings with the American Embassy. I taught at a Japanese Embassy school housed jointly with a French Embassy school. I was an adjunct professor at a major Russian university. Moreover, I had made friends with a Finnish woman who was married to a high-level British diplomat. He was so high level, in fact, that his Moscow office at the British Embassy had been bombed twice in as many months.

Now I am one of the least politically sophisticated people I know, but it seems my innocent higher-level connections with the Japanese, Canadians, Americans, Finns, Brits and Russians caused me to come under some scrutiny. Apparently—and I have this on good authority—I was being tailed on more than one occasion.

I've already mentioned what an abysmally poor sense of direction I have. I still pity the poor espionage agent assigned to follow me around on foot. Think of the frustration of tailing someone who could barely find her way to the trolley stop a half a block away. I can imagine this person cursing under his or her frozen breath as I made my umpteenth wrong turn en route to the Bolshoi Theater or got off yet again at the wrong Metro exit. ("Idiot, *idiyot, nyet!!* Turn left—*na leva, na leva. Nyet! Nyet! Nyet! Ne prava—na leva. Oy, k chorty!* Oh, to hell with it!")

How tempting it must have been for the spy to abandon cover, take me by the arm, and just personally guide me through the city, but that happened only twice, both times at Moscow's international airport, Sheremetovo. For those who have not been to Moscow, Sheremetovo, in the mid-1990s, was a drab concrete warehouse of a building seemingly illuminated by a single forty-watt bulb. No fast food places here. No telephones. No car rental kiosks. No friendly babushkas welcoming incoming tourists or saying goodbye to departing ones. Well, at least they had airplanes!

Although it was difficult to get into Russia, especially as a solo traveler, it was often more difficult to get out of Russia. Fees had to be paid, passports had to be inspected, re-inspected, and then held hostage by Intourist for a few weeks. Tickets had to be booked through an independent travel agency and then approved by the government. Furthermore, in order to get out of the country you needed an exit visa to let Russia know you were officially leaving.

Fortunately, all my documents were in order, but it seems the Soviet government was a little worried about my poor sense of direction. I was at Sheremetovo and had been cleared for passage on an Aeroflot flight to Los Angeles. I was waiting in a holding area to board the plane. After two hours we were told we would be allowed to board as soon as enough people had arrived to fill all the seats on the plane. No one could say how long that might be. Another hour or two, half a day, perhaps.

A pleasant young man approached and asked how my visit to Russia had been thus far. We had an interesting conversation and I thought he was just a friendly fellow traveler. It was a little suspicious, though, when later on he didn't board the plane along with me and everyone else. Still, in my naivete I didn't pay the encounter much notice. A year later, in January, 1997, the same young man met me at the same drab airport in Moscow.

"Do you remember me?" he asked. "I was here last year to see you off. We know you have a little trouble finding your way around. I'm here again this time just to make sure you get on the right plane and have a pleasant journey out of the country. "*Dasvidaniya* and Goodbye."

Episode Four
AT THE INVITATION OF CATHERINE THE GREAT

It was time to move from my shared two-room apartment in Moscow to a slightly larger and somewhat more private room. After three months, my landlady, her eight-year-old son and I were no longer compatible. The cat and I were still friends, fortunately. Mishka is the only cat I have ever met who was trained to use a regular toilet. Imagine my surprise when, in the middle of one dark night, I encountered two brightly shining eyes staring at me ten inches above the toilet seat. It was Mishka; I excused myself and let Mishka tend to business in privacy.

Finding a new apartment in Moscow was no easy matter, as living quarters were extremely hard to come by for several reasons. First, almost all apartments were occupied; there were years-long waiting lists of Russians who hoped to move from communal flats to private rooms. Second, Moscow was fast on its way to becoming one of the most expensive cities in the world; housing was especially expensive for a foreigner, particularly an American. Finally, there were no advertisements listing rooms for rent—everything was done through word of mouth.

Fortunately, before I left America an acquaintance had given me the name of a friend of a friend in Moscow who might be able to help me. Irina was an entrepreneurial computer programmer. She personally lived in a one-hundred-forty square foot flat with her husband and ten-year-old daughter. She shared a kitchen and bathroom with five other families. Despite her own less than ideal living conditions, Irina was willing to help find me someplace better to live. She did a bit of legwork, and we went out to inspect the room she had located.

Nadya and her daughter, Katya, lived in a "luxurious" three-room flat on the ground floor in a centrally located area of Moscow. Although it seemed that thirteen-year old Katya was less than ecstatic about sharing her living space, Nadya and her mother, referred to affectionately as Babushka, and Jerry the poodle were more enthusiastic. Nadya was a professor of ichthyology (fish studies) at the local scientific institute, but because of the Russian economic downturn, professors hadn't been paid a cent in over two years. Nadya needed some income, and hence her willingness to rent a room to me.

I was especially impressed by the large armoire in the rental room—someplace to put my gear instead of keeping it in my suitcases as I had been doing. The deal clincher, however, was the washing machine. Moscow had not a single detectable Laundromat in 1995, so I was delighted that I would be able to wash my Moscow-mud-splattered clothes with a mechanical device! We settled on the terms, and agreed that I would move in within the next two weeks in mid-March.

I mentioned to Nadya that, in addition to working in Russia and exploring the country, I was also looking for my family and doing genealogical research. I was really interested in going to Saratov, the largest city near Norka, where my birth family had lived. Turns out that Nadya had cousins with a vacant apartment in Saratov. Nadya contacted her family, and amazingly, although they had now known me for less than two hours, the family invited me to spend a few days alone in the Saratov apartment, rent free!

Irina and Nadya helped me get a train ticket to Saratov—no easy matter for Russians and even more difficult for foreigners with imperfect Russian. I was met in Saratov by Eugene, a young friend of the family, and he let me into the apartment. We had to dodge the laundry hanging out to dry on a clothesline in the living room. My room was filled with boxes, baskets, excess furniture, gardening tools, and five very large bags of potatoes. The kitchen sink, as it turned out, was right around the corner. The bed, however, was comfortable and the apartment was cheery and conveniently located near the trolley—well, almost atop the trolley tracks, actually. The jangle of the tram until two in the morning only added to the intrigue and anticipation.

Eugene accompanied me to the local government offices where we located the census records for the Saratov area, including ones for the Germans from Russia. The Germans from Russia, or *Ruskiy Nemtsiy,* were originally invited by Catherine the Great of Russia in 1763 to settle the area alongside the Volga River. Actually, she invited just about anyone to settle the sparsely populated area, but it was predominately the Germans who took her up on the offer. Catherine II wanted a community to act as a buffer against possible invading barbarians, and she offered the Germans free land, freedom from paying taxes, and freedom from conscription into military service in exchange for homesteading her territory. It seems I was a descendent of these settlers.

Dealing with bureaucracy is never easy, and it was particularly difficult in the Soviet Union. Still, Eugene and I convinced the census clerk that we should be allowed to look at the records for just a couple of minutes because, after all, I had come seven thousand miles to do so. In our brief survey of two or three pages of documents, we came across some Schwindts—so there were my people—officially enumerated among the inhabitants of Norka near Saratov!

I further met with the Mayor of Saratov, who, after listening to my story about the search for my roots, put a chauffeur and a Neva jeep at my disposal. The Neva jeep was quite luxurious, as it had been fitted with a proper exhaust system. Most Soviet vehicles of the time—or so it seemed to me—were designed so that the exhaust fumes flowed directly into the passenger compartment. That, plus the fact that so many Russians smoked, very nearly succeeded in asphyxiating the car's occupants. Not so in the well-ventilated jeep; what a luxury to be able to breathe the fresh country air of my ancestors.

Nikolai the chauffeur and I drove out to Norka (now known as Nekrasovo), which was about a three-hour drive from Saratov. It was March 9, 1995, not quite early spring, and the ground was still covered with snow. I had brought with me from America a copy of a map depicting Norka as it was in 1896. A distant relative had drawn this map by hand and from memory in 1921, long after emigrating from Russia to Canada in 1904. Nikolai and I did a bit of sleuthing and found the old *Ruskiy Nemtsiy* (German-Russian) cemetery. It had been pretty much destroyed by the Russians during World War II, as anti-German sentiment (even against those Germans who had lived in Russia for almost two hundred years) was very strong. We concluded our tour of Norka, a village of about three-hundred-fifty inhabitants, and I vowed to come back again.

Nikolai returned the Neva jeep to the office of the mayor and I was in for a very pleasant surprise. In honor of my continuing search for my roots, Mayor Alexander Bolokhnin had planned a small party for me in a local Saratov restaurant. True to Russian tradition the fete involved multiple toasts with Stolichnaya vodka as well as a sumptuous meal with several salads, caviar, borscht, fish, blini, Russian tortes and chocolate, followed by more toasts with vodka, brandy and champagne. At the end of the evening, Mayor Bolokhnin presented me with a book of historic photographs of Saratov, which he had inscribed: "Remember, Jill, about the days you spent in Saratov looking for your history. This is very touching—to look for truth from decades ago."

Episode Five

NARROW ESCAPES

I was all alone near Red Square and – big mistake! – I looked very much like a tourist. And, even bigger mistake! – I looked like an American tourist. On almost any other occasion, I would have congratulated myself on blending in with the Russians. By altering my stance, walk, gestures, and facial expressions I was almost never taken for an American. Opening my mouth to say something, of course, usually blew my cover and signaled that I was a foreigner in the midst of Muscovites.

Still, I had polished my Slavic accent well enough that Russians usually thought I was Polish; Poles thought I was Ukrainian; Ukrainians didn't bother to comment; and Czechs thought I was a misguided Russian. American tourists also seemed to think I was Russian, misguided or otherwise. On several occasions, when I answered their questions in English, Americans congratulated me on my surprisingly good command of the English language. They especially complimented me on my near mastery of an American accent. So, once again, Prince Charles: Take that!

I was, as I say, alone near Red Square. That in itself wouldn't have been cause for alarm, but I was blatantly, although unintentionally, playing the tourist. I had not just one, but two cameras ostentatiously strapped around my neck, one loaded with print film and the other with slide film. I was also carrying a shoulder bag. I had stopped to snap a few photos when an extended family of six or seven barefoot women and children appeared and began moving in on me. "*Tsgany*—Gypsies!!" shouted a Russian bystander who then scurried off in the opposite direction.

I had heard Russians tell tales about gypsies and their cunning at separating one from one's belongings. In extreme cases, Russians had warned me I could be beaten by these nomadic people who long ago, it is thought, migrated from India. I had decided these tales were exaggerated and used to justify discriminating against a poorly understood and much maligned minority. Besides, I had been quite intrigued with the gypsies' exotic appearance, colorful clothing and abundance of gold and silver jewelry. Now, as this bright-eyed, barefoot band quickly closed in on me, I thought there might be some truth to the warnings I had received.

I zigzagged back and forth across the street, increasing my pace. It soon became obvious that I was now too old to outrun anyone. With both my fear level and my heartbeat escalating, I continued zigging and zagging for several blocks. Finally, my pursuers got tired of dodging traffic and gave up the chase. That was the last time I conspicuously displayed any photo apparatus or other telltale signs of a self-absorbed, preoccupied tourist.

On another occasion I was with a group of about twelve friends from the Anglican Church in Moscow. We were en route to a social gathering when, all of a sudden, two or three gypsies cut me off from my pack of friends and began herding me like a calf away from the group. I was able to elude my followers and run back to my party, latching onto the arm of one of my friends and begging him not to let go until the danger was past. A couple of weeks earlier, another one of my friends from church had been knocked down and severely pummeled by a similar gypsy band; during the assault she injured her arm and suffered long-term damage to her vision.

Yet a third time I was walking with a Soviet Armenian acquaintance towards the Metro. We were approached by a man covetously eyeing our purses. We got into the Metro car; he got into the Metro car. We quickly got out; he quickly got out. We got back in; he got back in. We got out and ran into another car and left our would-be purse snatcher standing outside the railcar as the Metro took off. Whew!

One evening my landlady Nadya and I were at Moscow's first, and, at that time, only McDonald's. We were grabbing a bite to eat prior to seeing a performance, in Russian, of Neil Simon's *The Odd Couple*. Moscow's McDonald's was an immense place with a ground floor and a mezzanine and more than forty lines for ordering fast food. At that time, I was not yet a practicing vegetarian, so I can say on good authority that McDonald's Russian "gamburgers" and American hamburgers were indistinguishable, with the exception of the Cyrillic-printed packaging. We were lucky to find a place to sit down and Nadya was saving our seats while I ordered our meals. McDonald's, as always, was packed with people; it was winter, so it seemed even more jammed as everyone was bundled in heavy coats and boots.

I was bringing our French fries, Filet-o-Fishes, strawberry milkshakes and apple pies back to our table. I hadn't wanted to hold up the long line of fast-foodies by taking time to return my wallet to my purse; instead, trying to be polite, I had laid it temporarily on my food tray. During my transit from the order counter to our table, an elegant middle-aged woman clad in a full-length fur coat accidentally bumped into me. We apologized to one another and I made it back to our seats where Nadya and I consumed our dinners. When we got to the theater, I took out my wallet to buy our tickets to *The Odd Couple.* That is, I planned to take out my wallet, but it was nowhere to be found. Apparently, the elegant woman was in league with thieves and had purposely bumped into me to divert my attention and part me from my money. Well, she needed to pay for her fancy fur coat somehow.

A few days later I was on a mission to buy some English grammar books for my classes at the Japanese Embassy School. I had two hundred American dollars in cash in my purse as well as my prized Proof of Canadian Citizenship which I always carried for identification purposes. By then I no longer had my wallet, lost as it was in the encounter just described, but I did still have my shoulder bag. I was standing on a crowded trolley, trying to keep my balance. Two young men kept bumping into me making it more and more difficult to remain upright. Every time I rebalanced myself one or the other would bump into me from alternate sides. I was so busy trying to balance that I was only vaguely aware that my purse was being jostled.

I didn't want to draw attention to myself and risk having my imperfect accent proclaim my foreignness, so I said nothing. I continued to assume the duo was merely having a hard time keeping their footing—perhaps they'd been drinking. Finally, I alighted at my stop. I still had my shoulder bag securely draped over my right shoulder and tightly clutched in both hands, but it was now considerably lighter. It turns out the duo had slashed the bottom of my purse, removing not only my two hundred dollars, but more importantly, my Canadian Proof of Citizenship card.

Subsequently my purse was repaired, but I still had no wallet. A couple of days later my landlady Nadya and I headed off on a jaunt. While we were walking through an underpass, I encountered two of my young Japanese students. We exchanged greetings and during those few seconds I must have released my tight hold on my purse. It wasn't until a few hours later, when I went to apply some lipstick, that I realized my purse had once again been slashed. This time there was just a small hole. As I said, I hadn't yet replaced my wallet, so the thieves stole only my lipstick. I hope they liked the color.

While in Russia I travelled frequently by train. I love trains and I was quite lucky in my adventures on them; nothing dire happened to me although I did hear horror stories of other Americans and Russians being less fortunate than I. On one journey a young Russian woman and I boarded the train in Moscow and soon found ourselves sharing the same four-berth compartment. She and I congratulated one another on our luck at being two compatible women sharing the same berth. This was because solo passengers were destined to share the compartment overnight with three other travelers arbitrarily assigned by the Russian Railway.

Later in the evening two pleasant young Russian businessmen boarded our compartment and took the upper berths. The four of us exchanged names and learned more about one another. The two businessmen, Dmitri and Vladimir, warned us never to accept anything to drink—even in tightly sealed cans or bottles—from any unknown fellow traveler. Just the previous week, on another business journey, they had each made the mistake of accepting a can of soda from their compartment mates. Dmitri and Vladimir were soon out like lights and when they came to the next morning, they were minus all their money and other valuables. They speculated that the soda had been doctored with sedatives administered through the can with a hypodermic syringe. They further hypothesized that the train conductor was in on the scheme.

Dmitri and Vladimir warned us that occasionally, also with the seeming cooperation of the conductor, bandits would board the train at an appointed stop in the middle of the night. With everyone bedded down, and many of the passengers already asleep, the bandits quickly and quietly opened the doors to the compartments and sprayed some fast-acting sedative into the rooms. If I understood correctly, the spray was derived from belladonna and used as an anesthetic for cows. This was quite an effective get-rich scheme. Dmitri and Vladimir wanted to avoid any replay of this scenario, so they each removed their belts and spent about ten minutes securely wrapping them around our compartment door to keep unwanted visitors out. It was a little unnerving at first, as we had just met our travelling mates, and now we were locked inside the compartment with them. But everything turned out fine and we all woke up the next morning intact in body, soul and possessions.

I was remarkably lucky, actually, in my very limited encounters with crime. Oh sure, there was the time while I was shopping in the fashionable Arbat district when a Russian mafioso pulled out a gun. But I thought, what the heck, it's Russia, they do that here, the gun isn't pointed at me, and innocent bystanders don't get hurt. Very often. Fortunately, my luck held out. There was another more frightening time when a journalist was gunned down at the Pushkin Metro stop, but, by and large, I remained out of trouble.

The Arbat, by the way, is a pedestrian street in central Moscow dating back to at least the fifteenth century. Here, tourists and locals alike admire the elegant facades of buildings which line the half-mile-long cobblestone roadway. Pricy, high-quality Russian souvenirs can be found along the Arbat: You can buy an antique, pre-Revolutionary charcoal-fired brass samovar. If you don't want to bother with fire and smoke, you can instead choose a flamboyantly painted electric samovar. This samovar, translated from the Russian as "self-boiling", can now be used to heat water for brewing tea in your newly purchased Lomonosov teapot. The imperial Lomonosov porcelain factory was founded almost three hundred years ago by Catherine the Great, the daughter of Peter the Great. Lomonosov is still turning out fine hand-painted teacups from which to sip your tea.

While meandering down the Arbat you could, and still can, enjoy (or not) comedians, mimes, jugglers, trained and untrained dogs and all manner of musicians. One time I listened to a quintet of Peruvian flute players whose music was as mournful as their demeanor. You can also buy matryoshkas (the ubiquitous Russian nesting dolls); floral-patterned fringed scarves; balalaikas; lovely hand-painted ladies' watches; clunky Soviet issue men's Army watches; pirated CDs; enameled jewelry; miniature hand-carved wooden chickens, bears, fishes, troikas (three-horse sleighs); ceramics; and, in another price range altogether, exquisite lacquer boxes featuring scenes from Russian folktales, art, architecture or nature.

On one occasion I spotted a box depicting a brawny Soviet Mother-of-the-Year driving a tractor across her communal wheat field. Prior to the communist era, the lacquer box artists painted religious icons for the Russian Orthodox Church and its believers. The enterprising artists switched from icons to boxes when the Soviets outlawed the practice of religion. In 1996, the artform had gone full circle and, in addition to their boxes, the artists were once again painting religious icons.

But I digress. Aside from my wallet, Canadian documents, and lipstick, I lost only one other thing in my two years' stay in Russia. On one of my trips to the Czech Republic I had managed to pack lightly enough (a rarity for me then) so that everything fit into one carry-on-bag. Unfortunately, Czech Airlines wouldn't let me carry the carry-on-bag onto the plane, but made me check it in. It wasn't until a day later when I wanted to replenish the film in my camera that I found out someone had appropriated my twelve rolls of unexposed Fuji film.

On an earlier trip to Moscow in 1991, after I had arrived at my friend's home, happy but jetlagged, I attempted to open my suitcases. The first opened without a hitch, but the locking mechanism on the second refused to budge. I didn't know the Russian word for screwdriver, but after mutual gesturing, pantomime, pointing and gibberish, my friend provided me with the necessary tool.

It seems that customs had jimmied the lock to inspect the contents of the suitcase. Things were rearranged and messy, but everything still seemed to be intact. My Muscovite friend said it had to be **American** Customs who had opened the suitcase, because **Russian** Customs officials would have treated the contents as on-the-job perks and divvied up the good stuff among themselves.

During Soviet times, when people in the West sent gifts to their friends and family back in Russia, they devised creative methods to try to cut down on pilfering. If, for example, they were sending a pair of shoes, the left shoe went into one package and the right shoe into another package. The two packages would then be shipped at least a week apart, thus making it less likely that a customs officer would bother to pilfer just one shoe.

Tipping, as such, wasn't really practiced in Russia, but "gift giving" was. In Russia in 1995, a one-dollar bill was considered a very generous gift for someone who had performed a service such as driving a taxi or guiding a tour. Lipstick also made a nice gift for a woman as did a pair of costume jewelry earrings. For a man, a bottle of vodka was a highly prized gift, but it was far more cumbersome to carry about than a one-dollar bill. For my extended stay in Russia I decided to take one hundred one-dollar bills for such gift giving niceties and necessities.

Rather than carry a thick wad of money in my purse or in my around-the-neck money/passport holder, I decided to put my one hundred one-dollar bills in an envelope in my suitcase. Although I really didn't want to have them stolen, I reasoned that I would rather lose them from my suitcase than from my person. Also, someone seeing a one-inch thick wad of folding money might assume it was several thousand dollars rather than a hundred dollars. I believe I made the right decision. My money arrived safely, and I wasn't mugged. *Schastliviye puteshestviya!* Safe travels.

Episode Six
CHEERS!

My new landlady, Nadya, and I had become good friends. I had seen the towns of Norka and Saratov in March, 1995, and now wanted to see them in summer. Nadya's relatives lived in Saratov, not too far from Norka, so we decided to visit them in the summer of 1995. We stayed for two-and-a-half weeks, soaking up the sun, swimming in the Volga, visiting churches, shopping at bazaars, feasting on locally grown apricots and generally enjoying the company and hospitality of Nadya's cousins.

Of course, I had my heart set on seeing Norka at least one more time, so I headed to the office of the Mayor of Saratov. Mayor Bolokhnin remembered me from my solo visit five months ago in March. For a second time he put a Neva jeep at my disposal, as well as Nikolai, the same chauffeur who had shown me Norka in early springtime.

Nikolai was an excellent driver and a very pleasant companion, and he and I, and Nadya this time as well, set out once again for the birthplace of all four of my grandparents. In the mid to late 1800s Norka (which means mink in Russian) had had a population of eight thousand to ten thousand people. Now, in 1995, the population had dwindled to a mere three-hundred-fifty inhabitants or so. There were televisions but no telephones. Rich soil, but almost no agriculture except for small garden plots. Electricity and running water, but no indoor baths or toilets. There were horse-drawn carts but only one or two cars. No obvious shops, library, restaurant, gas station, seed and feed suppliers or any other signs of commerce. Definitely no supermarket, which at that time was not to be found even in Moscow. There was one small government office housing a telegraph service and post office. But there was no one on duty that day, nor likely on the day before nor the day to come. And the only traffic jam we encountered was a bevy of ducks and geese taking a very long time to waddle from one side of a narrow dirt road to the other.

Nikolai, Nadya and I did a bit of detective work to try to find a few Germans from Russia, *Ruskiy Nemtsiy*, still living in Norka. The vast majority of the German-Russian population had been dispersed during Stalin's reign, either to Siberia or to Kazakhstan. The Russian government had only recently allowed some *Ruskiy Nemtsiy* to return to the Russian towns that their relatives had called home for more than two hundred years. One family, the Adlers, had returned from Kazakhstan two years previously and were hoping ultimately to emigrate to Germany.

Lily and Basil Adler and their daughters, Katya, five; Olga, seven; and Irina, twelve, lived in a home built around the time of Catherine the Great of Russia—more than two centuries ago. The interior had been updated and was bright and cheery with freshly laundered sheer white lacy curtains at the windows. A repurposed vodka bottle, filled with wildflowers from the garden, decorated the kitchen table. Russian folk art, one or two icons, and photographs from out-of-date calendars hung from the brick façade of the interior walls.

Lily and Basil were typical Russian hosts, and, as such, celebrated our impromptu visit with an improvised feast of soup, salads, bread and vodka—especially vodka. In Russia it is considered very poor manners to abstain from a toast and equally poor manners to set your glass down without consuming its contents in one glug. If you don't quickly drink each glassful of alcohol in its entirety, you invalidate not only the sentiments of the toast, but you insult both the giver and the recipient of that toast as well.

Nikolai the chauffeur, being a true professional driver, abstained from all toasts and liquor for that day. Basil, Lily, Nadya and I, on the other hand, toasted one another and everything at every imaginable opportunity. We offered toasts for nature, birch trees, squirrels, rivers, sunshine; for borscht, blini, sour cream and kefir; for villages, towns, cities, and countries; for literature and music and art—with collective good cheer to Tolstoy, Chekhov, Dostoevsky, Dickens, Edgar Allen Poe, James Fennimore Cooper, and Mark Twain; thanks also to Mozart, Mendelsohn, Tchaikovsky, Beethoven, and the Beatles; hooray for Matisse, Monet, Levitan, Renoir and Rembrandt; and, above all, cheers to enduring comradery, friendship, love and peace. By now we had consumed a lot a vodka!

When we were ready to say farewell to the Adlers, Nadya was barely upright, and Nikolai, being the only one steady on his feet, helped her to the car. Sitting in the back seat of the Neva jeep, my giddy friend and I enjoyed our three-hour ride back to Saratov. We drove past several large fields filled with sunflowers, all tilting their happy faces upwards and facing the same westerly direction as they followed the late afternoon's solar rays. Once, Nikolai ran into a field and snatched one of the beautiful giant yellow blooms for us to enjoy as an edible souvenir.

When we arrived at our apartment, Nadya had forgotten her address, phone number, and just about everything but her name. Nikolai assisted her to our room and she immediately careened into bed, moaning occasionally about her splitting headache. I seemed to be doing a bit better. I decided to freshen up, brush my teeth and go for a walk. I had a little trouble navigating the rutted streets and responding to people who greeted me, but nonetheless enjoyed myself. Nadya moaned and groaned throughout the night and on into the next morning, until she finally pulled herself together and got out of bed. She was particularly upset that I, the American, had fared better than she, the Russian: *"Shto eto takoy?* The *Amerikanka* came home, brushed her teeth, went for a walk, and never even had a headache! *Pravda!"*

Before we said goodbye, the Adlers had invited me to return to Norka on my own and visit them. It was an open invitation; hence, no firm date was set. This was an opportunity I couldn't pass up, so, on August 3, 1995, I set out by myself on a bus bound for Norka. There was no way to let the Adlers know I was coming, as neither they nor anyone in the village had a telephone.

The bus from Saratov to Norka ran every other day. It was packed with local people carrying fruits and vegetables, dogs, cats, ducks, chickens, children, shovels, rakes, and small bags full of grain. Although there was standing room only, and just barely that, I, as the only foreigner, was given the place of honor. They cleared a small niche for me just behind the driver, and I shoehorned myself in next to an amiable heavy-set babushka, her shy young granddaughter, and their half dozen chickens in a woven reed basket. The trip lasted several hours, and as we got closer to our destination, all of the passengers still onboard, including the four-legged ones, were finally able to sit down.

We arrived in Norka and the bus driver asked if I knew where the Adlers lived. No, I didn't know exactly, but I figured that in a village of only three-hundred-fifty, someone would be able to direct me. "Hey, you! *malchikiy!*" the driver shouted to a couple of kids on the street. "Show this American where she wants to go."

Without too much trouble I arrived unannounced at the Adlers'. Seems they hadn't let up on their drinking since the previous time we were there. In fact, the entire village seemed to be under the influence of alcohol. Drinking, apparently, was the primary, if not the only, form of entertainment. *Bozhe!* What had I let myself in for?! The bus was long gone, and the next one wouldn't be along for two days. There were no telephones, no taxis and no way out.

I needn't have worried. Everyone treated me with warmth and generosity and dignity. In fact, an intoxicated Basil Adler knocked on the door of my guest room and said he wanted to tell me something. His slurred speech made it more difficult than usual for me to understand Russian. Nevertheless, Basil wanted to assure me that, even though he knew he was quite drunk, he would in no way "bother" me in the middle of the night. He repeated this several times and then, to reinforce his point, showed me how to lock the door to my room. Basil was true to his word and remained a perfect gentleman.

As an adoptee, the first time I met anyone from my birth family occurred nearly half a century after I was born. Serendipitously, two of my newly discovered Canadian cousins turned out to be the dedicated keepers of their—and hence **my**—family tree, records, history, and memorabilia. During my visit to Canada to meet them for the first time, my relatives, knowing that I had plans to travel to Russia soon, gave me a map of Norka. This map had been drawn by hand and from memory in 1927 by a then ninety-year-old relative. It showed her town as she remembered it from childhood, during the mid-1800s.

Now, back in Norka and with this map in hand, I located the family home of my paternal Grandfather Schwindt. The home was still standing and in quite good repair. The exterior of the three-foot-thick walls was dark natural wood, and the windows had been trimmed with my favorite color, light blue. The current occupant invited me in and I was able to see where my grandfather and great grandfather Schwindt had been born and lived until they left in 1900 to homestead their farms in Canada. An additional new rotund wood-fired stove had been added to operate in tandem with the earlier stove to ward off the Russian winter cold.

The children of the village gave me a grand tour. Using my hand drawn map for reference, we visited the "new" school of 1916, no longer in use. I saw where the beehives had been kept one hundred years ago. A few scrawny dead trees marked the spot of the former apple orchard. I came upon the stone quarry and the gravel pit and the old mill. I photographed the exterior of the old German church and saw where the courthouse had once stood. I revisited the partially destroyed cemetery for the Germans from Russia and, by crawling under a few bushes, was able to photograph some remaining headstones to later show my people in Canada. Directionally challenged or not, I was able to pinpoint the various family homes depicted on my map, and I spent two peaceful days soaking up the atmosphere in Norka, the village where my paternal and maternal grandparents and their extended families had been born.

Episode Seven
NEVER TAKE NYET FOR AN ANSWER

I had been in Russia almost a year. To renew my visa, which was soon to expire, I had to exit Russia, travel to a foreign nation, and visit the Russian embassy there. Bureaucracy was alive and well in the world's largest country, and red tape was directly proportional to geographic size. Only outside her far-reaching borders could miniscule details be evaluated, questioned, argued, rebutted or refuted. On the rare occasion when approval might be forthcoming, there would appear a self-congratulatory government official directly descended from one of Nikolai Gogol's political satires of the mid-1800s. *The Inspector General* comes to mind.

If one was fortunate, the civil servant would meticulously inspect the document, deliberately nod his or her approval, cough once, make one final flourish with the pen and then sign the paperwork. After pausing for effect, this clerk would produce a key, retrieve a wood-handled stamp from a tiny locked compartment of a nearby enormous apothecary cabinet, apply the rubber stamp to an indigo-hued stamp pad, slowly bring the now-inked rubber stamp into contact with the bottom right corner of each page of the document, and, in so doing, impose the requisite insignia of bureaucratic authority. Yes, under Tsars and Soviets, Gorbachev and Yeltsin—officialdom remained secure.

With any luck, and by following the aforementioned time-honored process, a contemporary embassy official might agree to renew **my** document, and I could then extend my Russian stay for another six months. If the embassy official denied my request, I would have to return posthaste to Moscow, gather up my belongings, and leave the country within two weeks, before my current visa expired on January 5, 1996.

Thankfully, Babushka—the mother of my friend and landlady, Nadya, had friends in Tallinn, the capital of Estonia. I took the overnight train to Tallinn in late December, 1995, and checked into a small hotel. While in Eastern Europe, I never had the luxury of travelling five-star, and generally stayed in one-and-a-half-star accommodations. This hotel was a step above and rated at least two-and-a-quarter stars. Although out of necessity I always chose cheap accommodations, I required them to be safe, and clean as well. Quiet was a definite perk, and having a bathroom to oneself was enough to rate another star.

The next day, Babushka's friends, Kaljo Alakula and his son, Kristjan, met me at my hotel and drove us to the Russian Embassy. There, an official notice posted on the locked door announced the Embassy's closure for the day. Why hadn't one of us made a phone inquiry prior to setting out that morning? Because in the dissolving Soviet Union there were still **no** phone directories and, hence, **no** directory assistance. If you or your friends didn't know the number, you were in the dark until you showed up in person at your destination. That is, if you could learn the address from someone. In Tallinn, unlike Moscow, there were thin, rudimentary, dogeared phone directories, but the Embassy's number wasn't listed.

So, the three of us changed tack and headed for the Alakulas' beautiful architect-designed home with its view of the Baltic Sea; clearly they had done quite well under the previous Soviet regime. Mrs. Alakula prepared an impromptu lunch of elegantly sliced sandwiches for the four of us. After a visit that lasted several hours, Kristjan kindly chauffeured me around for some sightseeing and then returned me to my hotel just prior to sunset. From my humble, sparsely-furnished and minimally-decorated room I began making plans to renew my visa on the following day. That is, if the embassy was open.

Early the next morning, Kristjan drove me to the Russian Embassy which, Hooray! *Slava Boga!* was now open for business. Kristjan dropped me off; I got into the line which extended for about a block outside the building and prepared to wait. And wait, and wait . . . and wait. Although it was December, the weather, fortunately, was still fall-like and it hadn't yet snowed that winter.

By noon, having finally made it inside the Embassy, I was now meeting with Svetlana, a minor bureaucrat who would decide my fate. She spoke Russian very rapidly and I had great difficulty comprehending. It was clear Svetlana wasn't going to cut me any slack. Too bad I was having a hard time understanding her, she commented sarcastically, but I was an American who had likely taken a job away from one of her compatriots. Now I would suffer the consequences. Besides, if I was smart enough to teach English at the University, I should be smart enough to converse fluently in **her** native language.

Svetlana officiously informed me that my visa would quite likely not be renewed, at least if she had any say in the matter. It seems that on the previous day the American Embassy had tightened its restrictions on Russians obtaining American visas, and now Svetlana (and her government) decided that turnabout was fair play. Apparently, I was to be the first scapegoat. No, I couldn't have a visa, it didn't matter that I taught at Moscow State University, it was irrelevant that I really wanted to remain in the country and fulfill my work commitment, the answer was *nyet*, no, no, no. Besides, they were closing for lunch break.

As the lengthy line along the sidewalk began to disperse, I tried to remain calm and plan my strategy for the upcoming two-hour lunch recess. I hurriedly walked to the American Embassy where the staff responded: "What do you expect **us** to do? You came to this country on your own; you'll need to solve this problem on your own." As a dual citizen, I also visited the Canadian Embassy a few blocks away. The friendlier Canadians tried to assist, made a few calls to the Russian officials, but met with no success. They also let me spend time in the embassy building, where they gave me some homemade cookies and maple-flavored tea, and allowed me to warm up.

Thus fortified, I returned to the Russian Embassy and prepared to wage my peaceful assault. Oh, no! I was now about a block away, and I could see that people were rapidly reassembling and jostling one another to claim an advantageous spot. I had failed to realize this was likely to happen. When I arrived, the line already reached the end of the block and was beginning to snake around the corner. On the spur of the moment I calculated where my previous place would have been before lunch, if the line hadn't dispersed. Then in my most authentic Soviet manner—that is, somber, unapologetic, rude and determined—I wedged myself into the ever-lengthening queue of Russians and took my place among the crowd. I ignored my comrades who were shoving, glaring, swearing, gesticulating, and tsk-tsking their overall disapproval of my Soviet demeanor.

During this crushing experience, the ballpoint pen in my purse snapped in two. I, on the other hand, dug in the heels of my tractor-tread boots and held my ground. It was now beginning to snow, and by the time I entered the building for a second time that day, the snow was up to my ankles. Beautiful as it was, I was happy to be out of it.

I vowed not to leave the building until I had an answer. Svetlana, the minor bureaucrat, did everything she could to discourage me, but I held firm. She let me remain and said I might be able to meet with a more senior official. At 4:57 p.m. everyone was ordered out of the building, as it was time to close for the day. I insisted on meeting with my promised official. I was the lone foreigner in a nearly empty Russian Embassy. The possibility of my being snatched, blindfolded, loaded into a *Moskvitch* sedan and "disappeared" by the government crossed my mind. Amazingly, the two guards let me stay, and I finally did get to meet with a higher-level bureaucrat by the name of Ivan Ivanovich Pavlov. He said there was nothing he could do that day, but might possibly be able to assist me tomorrow if I came by during his lunch hour at 1 p.m.

I phoned my Estonian acquaintance, Kristjan, and he agreed to meet me the next day and see if he could do anything to help. I spent a sleepless night knowing that without my visa I'd be heading back to America in two weeks, leaving my coveted jobs, friends, and fascinating Russian life behind.

Early next morning, Kristjan gave me a second tour of Tallinn, including vistas of the Baltic Sea. Of course, as a Southern Californian I'd seen the ocean on multiple occasions, and as an expat living in Eastern Europe, I'd seen plenty of snow. This was the first time I'd ever seen snow and sea combined, as the luminous white flakes fell onto the gently rolling, nearly frozen, slushy gray-blue waves.

At the appointed time—just three hours before my train would depart for Moscow—Kristjan delivered me to the Russian Embassy. Kristjan met briefly with the official I was to see, but he was told I would be on my own—no interpreters or friends allowed. I nervously entered the office of Ivan Ivanovich Pavlov. He placed some documents before me and asked if I could translate them. I answered that I could, but likely not very well. He said it would have to do. He interviewed me in Russian for about thirty minutes, and then said he had one final question and that receiving my visa depended upon my answer. I nervously awaited his all-important question.

"There is something about the English language that I have always found puzzling," he said. As an English teacher, I was hopeful I would be able to respond appropriately to his question: "What is the difference in meaning and pronunciation between the name for a man's three-piece business outfit; a small group of rooms in a hotel; and the taste of something you might eat for dessert?" I am happy to say that my English proficiency and my ability to differentiate between "suit," "suite," and "sweet" earned me my visa and the right to remain another half year in Mother Russia.

The next time my visa was due to expire, in June, 1996, I decided to fly to Prague, the lone American among a group of thirty-nine Russians. We were met at the Czech airport by Ladislav, our bilingual tour leader. I asked Ladislav if he also spoke English; he didn't and was puzzled that I had asked the question. I explained that English was my first language and it would be easier for me to communicate in that language rather than Russian. It seems that I had fooled him into thinking I was a native Russian speaker. Flattering as that may sound, it didn't always work to my benefit.

Apparently, my accent was good enough that, for a short time at least, I was able to pass as Russian. If people spoke to me a little longer, they thought I might be Polish or Lithuanian, but they didn't usually detect an American accent. Unfortunately, my grammar was nowhere near as good as my accent, so I would often find myself conversing with a suddenly bemused and occasionally offended Russian who couldn't figure out why, if I had had a standard Soviet education, my language skills were so substandard.

Now we were in Prague. With its medieval Charles Bridge spanning the meandering Vltava River; and its steep and narrow winding lanes edged by small shops which have been in business for the past one thousand years; and its six-hundred-year-old astronomical clock which still keeps accurate time while simultaneously displaying the celestial bodies **and** the Twelve Apostles, Prague is the most beautiful city I have ever visited.

And I haven't even mentioned the classical music concerts taking place every summer night at elegant historic venues around the city; whimsical toys, lithographs, satirical puppets, greeting cards and other fun items available from the artists who create them; Prague Castle and St. Vitus Cathedral perched on a steep hill but easily accessible via the municipal tram; and architecture which is so exquisite from every angle that I soon stopped taking photographs and simply stood in awe and admiration.

Prague is also closely associated with my favorite composer, Mozart. I was able to visit Bertramka, a country villa and vineyard on the outskirts of the city; Mozart spent some time here with his hosts, the Duseks, also musicians, and it is here that he completed his opera, *The Marriage of Figaro*.

I saw a performance of *Figaro* at the Estates Theatre in Prague; it was at this same theatre, on October 29, 1787, that Mozart personally conducted the premiere performance of another of his operas, *Don Giovanni*. But for me, the best part of Bertramka was to come face to face with Mozart's very own piano, with its finely patinaed wood and its lustrous white keys. Several guest artists were on a rotating schedule, and they were invited to play frequently. This was not just for the enjoyment of the pianist and the audience. Regularly playing the instrument helped keep the piano's sound quality as identical as possible to what Mozart might have heard in his day, more than two hundred years ago.

As I mentioned earlier, I was the lone American traveling with thirty-nine Russians and one Czech tour guide on our excursion to Prague. Most of my fellow traveling companions were well mannered and sensitive to the fact that not all Czechs welcomed former Soviets with open arms. The subtleties of political correctness were lost, however, on a few of the Nouveau Riche Russians among us. Several of these Nouveaux advised me that they, as well as I, would be speaking only English while on our trip. They would, they explained, be spending hundreds, if not thousands of US dollars as they filled many, many suitcases with coveted Czech crystal in order to impressively decorate their Moscow McMansions and country dachas. They did not want to be identified immediately as ostentatious Russians while they invaded the small shops of artisans for crystal chandeliers, goblets, vases and other shimmering treasures. Much better that they pass themselves off as rich Americans whom the Czechs would more likely welcome with open arms and open cash registers, or so they reasoned. Who can say? This deception might have succeeded if the big spenders had known just a little bit more than a paragraph's worth of English.

A particularly obnoxious fellow seemed to delight in embarrassing his family and the rest of us, proclaiming at every opportunity, *"Ya Ruskiy! Ya Ruskiy!* I'm Russian! Pay attention to me! I demand immediate service!"

One evening the forty of us set out for Krizik, a fountain of three thousand water jets illuminated by twelve-hundred underwater multicolored spotlights. Music—classical, popular, folk, electronic, movie and Broadway show tunes—accompanied high-reaching and far-ranging waterspouts which coordinated spectacularly with scintillating displays of light. We had arrived by trolley at the farthest corner of the park which had housed the 1891 Prague Exhibition. It was dusk and getting darker. It was also raining cats and dogs. The rainwater was several inches deep in some of the flooded areas en route to the fountains. From our group of forty, thirty-five of us took the deluge with good humor, dodging puddles and appreciating the irony of travelling to see a manmade water show while in the midst of a more spectacular natural one.

The main gate to the arena was flooded out from the rain, so we had to walk about two blocks to another entrance. The Really Obnoxious *Mister Ruskiy* was having none of it! He stood at the entrance to the main gate with his wife and three children and shouted at the top of his lungs, *"Ya Ruskiy.* I'm Russian. Let me in."

This did not go over well with the Czechs, and, really obnoxious or not, the gate remained closed to him and his family.

Thirty-four relatively dry Russians and I made our way through the alternate gate and took our seats. We thoroughly enjoyed the spectacular display of illuminated water and classical music, punctuated as it was by an occasional "I'm Russian; I'm rich, and I want some service now!" A soggy *Mister Ruskiy* finally squish-squished his way into the bleachers. By the time he realized he wasn't going to receive special treatment, he was drenched to the bone, and he and his family sat huddled together at the far reaches of the arena, quiet at last.

Episode Eight
A WEIGHTY DILEMMA

Christine was about half my age, and at two-hundred-fifty pounds, she was more than double my size. We both taught English at Moscow State University on Monday and Wednesday evenings, but other than seeing one another twice a week outside our nearby classrooms, we had no further association. Still, it seemed we'd be adequately compatible for a joint four-day excursion to Warsaw, and we agreed that it was easier to travel with someone than to travel solo. Usually.

Things started out well enough. *The Moscow Journal*, the expat biweekly newspaper, had assured us that, even without advance reservations, we would have no problem whatsoever finding accommodations in Warsaw and later on in the medieval Polish town of Krakow. And I tried hard not to let the fact that Christine had several tattoos and spiky maroon hair affect my opinion of her as a traveling companion.

Moscow has nine train stations, each one of them conveniently located near a Metro stop. Not so conveniently, in Russia's capital city in 1996, there were no listed phone numbers because there were no phone directories. No printed pocket-sized, or any-sized train schedules. No available fax numbers. And, because it was pre-digital, no email, Google, smart phones, GPS or map apps. Hence, an in-person visit to a virtual ticket counter became necessary. Since Christine and I would be travelling through Belarus en route to Poland, we set out for the appropriately named *Belorusskiy* (Belorussian) train station.

And here at last, encircling an immense marble column, we found posted a hand-printed flimsy cardboard schedule with a variety of connections between Moscow, Minsk, Warsaw, Prague, Vienna, Berlin, and Paris. The heavily smudged, dog-eared chart/schedule, such as it was, featured multiple hand-written corrections, cross-outs, addenda, footnotes, color-coded references, and other bureaucratic complexities seemingly understood only by the ticket cashier and the director of the Russian passenger railway system.

Oh, yes, and apparently by Christine. My self-assured American colleague was infinitely more adept than I, and even some Russians, at decoding the schedule and purchasing two one-way tickets from Moscow to Warsaw for the pair of us. One-way, because round-trip would likely have been too practical for the Soviets, whose system required us to acquire the return trip ticket after our arrival in the foreign country to which we were travelling.

Our departure was scheduled for the next day from the Belorussian train station. Of the nine rail terminals in Moscow, this one, completed in 1870, was the sixth. Painted an unexpected, but lovely, pastel blue-green and trimmed in white, this terminal held its own history. In 1896, Nicholas II, Russia's last Tsar, and his wife Alexandra, arrived at this station for their coronation within Moscow's Kremlin walls at the Assumption Cathedral. The same place where, in 1547, Ivan the Terrible had been crowned the first Tsar of all Russia. The Easter-egg-colored terminal was also closely linked to both World War I and World War II, as troops and supplies departed to the front, and the wounded returned to Moscow via the same route.

The next day, Christine and I arrived at the station and boarded our train to Poland. At the start of our journey, we travelled in a non-compartmentalized train car with hard wooden-slatted benches for seats. These sit-where-you-will accommodations were not particularly comfortable, but on this train, they were clean, and there were many vacant benches from which to choose. Thank goodness, no need to stand for several hours as was so often the case on jam-packed commuter trains.

Russian public conveyances, including railway and Metro trains, streetcars and trolley buses, were often so crowded that, while standing, it was possible to plant not two, but only one foot firmly on the floor. Finding a handhold was not an option, and exiting often required getting off at a stop other than the one you wanted. Speaking from experience, you are well advised not to carry a peanut butter and jelly sandwich in your pocket or purse. Don't even think about eggs.

And, because Christine and I had departed from a large city, we had been able to walk directly from the platform onto the train. Stops in the countryside usually lacked any kind of elevated areas alongside the tracks. There, passengers were dependent upon strong and charitable souls willing to hoist them up from the ground to the floor of the train car. Along with their packages, sacks of home-grown produce, babies and children, fishing apparatus, and whoever and whatever else might be travelling. Disembarking required pretty much the same process in reverse, unless you were fearless and decided to jump three or more feet from the car directly onto the ground.

About an hour into the journey, four very muscular young Russian men boarded our train car. Each member of the quartet was dressed in oversized pants and ill-fitting, long-sleeved jackets and looked like he had spent far too much time working out unsupervised at the gym (or, more likely, harvesting potatoes). Although there were still plenty of seats available, they remained standing.

Minutes after our train had exited the station, the four young men opened their backpacks, pulled out hammers, pliers, screw drivers and monkey wrenches, and immediately set to work dismantling the light fixtures. None of our fellow passengers appeared dismayed, puzzled or concerned, so Christine and I remained nonchalant as well.

When they had finished their "renovation" they stripped off their jackets and pants, displaying bottles of vodka duct-taped to their torsos and legs. After removing their bootlegged cache from their bodies, they quickly hid it inside the light fixtures, and within minutes had put the train compartment back to normal. They secreted their carpentry tools in their backpacks, put their pants and jackets on again, took their seats, and settled in.

Christine, sitting on the bench opposite me, went back to reading her well-worn paperback romance novel, which, on its front cover, featured a raven-haired damsel in distress wearing a ripped bodice of scarlet velvet. I decided now would be a good time to catch up on my sleep. I removed my shoes, put my stockinged feet up on my bench and stretched out. But not for long. No sooner had I closed my eyes and started to doze, than the conductor came by. She was not amused and swatted my feet, hips and face with a newspaper.

"Nyet, nyet! Nilza! It is forbidden to lie down on the benches!"

Hmmm . . . bootlegging yes, napping no.

About fifteen minutes before our arrival in Belarus, customs officials boarded the train, made a thorough inspection of our car and found nothing amiss. They checked our documents, and cleared us all for entry into their country. As soon as the customs officials exited the train our four bootleggers set to work again, dismantling the light fixtures, fishing out their vodka bottles, removing their outer clothing, and hastily taping their loot to their bodies. Thus bulked up, they slipped into their pants, threw on their jackets, and, once again, looked like they should consider cancelling their gym membership, or at least hire a new personal trainer. They then repaired the lights, returned everything to normal and we all disembarked at the next stop. Free enterprise was definitely making a comeback in Mother Russia.

Christine and I, along with other passengers continuing on through Belarus into Poland, now needed to board an overnight train. We were assigned a sleeper compartment with four bunks, Christine in the upper, opposite a very handsome young Russian male, and I in the lower, opposite a not so handsome young Russian man. Christine immediately turned on the charm and utilized all the flirting techniques she more than likely had honed while reading her romance novel earlier. Within twenty minutes, I had the compartment to myself as Christine, Boris and Igor headed to the bar for a few shots of vodka.

Before too long, the not so handsome Boris returned to settle in for the night. Christine, behind him, stuck her head through the doorway and announced that she and the very handsome Igor were going to a more private location to gaze at the constellations. But not before she had demanded that Boris relocate immediately to an upper bunk so that she could have his more convenient lower one upon her return.

In an hour or so, stargazing apparently over, Christine and Igor stumbled into our cabin. Boris, as previously requested by Christine, was now in the bunk above mine, likely asleep. I also had been asleep until Christine thrust her fist above my face to bang on the bottom of Boris's bunk, demanding that he now descend once again to his previous lower bunk opposite mine. That way, she and Igor, *inamorati* that they now were, could hold hands across the aisle while romantically ensconced in their two upper bunks. Having thus rearranged all passengers to her satisfaction, Christine told me to face the wall, keep my eyes, ears and mouth shut and go to sleep so the tryst could continue in relative privacy. Such were our travels across Belarus in the middle of the night.

Well before dawn, the conductor rattled our cabin door and advised us four that we would disembark very soon in Brest, Belarus. Passengers continuing into Poland would first need to obtain appropriate documents which could be had from a lone Belarussian official housed in a kiosk "somewhere in the train station". A more precise location was not forthcoming.

Christine was barely on speaking terms with the good-looking Igor this morning, so it was just as well that he and Boris would be boarding a different train from ours and heading to parts unknown. Half-hearted farewells were said, and then Christine and I set out in the pre-dawn darkness to search for the mysterious government kiosk. Following our instincts, we immediately headed for the longest line in the terminal and took our places behind the forty plus travelers already there. It seems all of us would need to purchase an exit visa to get ourselves out of Belarus. Well, we knew the Belarussians wouldn't take Russian currency, but a couple of Russians offered to exchange their Belarussian money for some of our US dollars. There, that was easy. Problem solved!

As the sun began just poking above the horizon, the corrugated metal window of the kiosk slowly opened. Our fellow travelers began passing along the necessary forms which we completed while waiting. After about forty-five minutes we came face to face with an unsmiling representative of the government of Belarus. We handed him our signed forms, and our Russian and American documents, and prepared to hand him a wad of Belarussian money as well.

"*Nyet, nyet*, no good," he said.

From our purses we extracted yet another wad of his country's legal tender.

"*Nyet, nyet*, no good. Understand? *Panimayete?* Belarus money no good in Belarus. No good Russian, no good Polish, no good Ukrainian, all money no good. German money good. US money good. You have Deutschmarks, US dollars? *Da?*"

Well, yes, fortunately we did. So, after completing our transactions with US currency, we were soon back on the train and heading once again towards Poland. But not for long. Another stop, another government official—this one Polish—another inspection of our documents and another stamp on our passports. At last, we crossed over the border into Poland en route to our final destination now four hours away.

Christine, flinging around her fifty-pound backpack like it was a small tote bag, and I, struggling with my lightweight weekender, had just arrived at the Warsaw travelers aid kiosk. Bystanders probably thought I looked like a disgruntled, bedraggled, hungry, hot and sweaty, travel-weary middle-aged school teacher. They were right. Christine, unfazed by our travels and even more raucous than usual, was sporting several body piercings and brightly-colored tattoos which complemented her spiky maroon hair. She was wearing low cut jeans which set off her ample spare tire to best advantage. And the ring in her navel, an accessory I had not noticed before, sparkled in the Eastern European sunlight.

The effect was not lost on the travel assistant at the kiosk who eyed us both from head to toe, toe to head, and then from head to toe again. Regrettably, she informed us, there were no reasonably priced double rooms to be had. In fact, the agent was able to find just one available room in all of Warsaw. But, as she explained in Polish, pantomime, and artistic doodles, it contained only one very long and narrow European-style single bed.

While Christine and I were pondering what to do, our chances of renting that one remaining room evaporated. This time the agent, foregoing Polish, and utilizing just pantomime and doodles, clearly pointed out that our combined weights of approximately 165 kilograms exceeded the load limit and would produce unnecessary stress on the furnishings. A drawing of a collapsed bed emphasized her point.

We had reached an impasse. What to do? Christine, ever resourceful, especially when it worked to her benefit, hit upon a plan.

She had an ex-boyfriend from Warsaw, Pavel, who was presently out of the country. She had had the foresight to bring the phone number for Pavel's mother, Sonia, for just such an emergency. Christine said she would feel a twinge of guilt, but only slight, as she would need to convince Sonia that she and Pavel were not exes, but had reconciled. In fact, she would enthusiastically insinuate that they were still a devoted, albeit long-distance, romantic couple.

My oversized companion phoned Sonia and charmed her would-be future mother-in-law into coming to pick us up from our current location at the travel bureau. Sonia spoke no English and minimal Russian, and we spoke no Polish; nonetheless, we managed to communicate in the two somewhat-related Slavic languages. Sonia was a warm and friendly hostess and seemed delighted that her son Pavel once again had an enterprising American girlfriend. She said that she had an extra apartment where we could spend a few nights. The apartment was currently undergoing renovations, and the only drawback, Sonia said, was the bed. There was just one—a twin. Not to worry; we'd work something out.

Christine's charm was short-lived and lasted just until Sonia dropped us off at our new temporary accommodations. My colleague then became more and more overbearing and obnoxious, pushing her abundant weight around to underscore her point. Later in the day while we were buying some sweet rolls from a street vendor, she knocked me off my feet when she quickly turned around and unexpectedly clouted me with her mammoth backpack. It may have been an accident but I've never been entirely convinced. At the very least, she needn't have been so dismissive and short-tempered when she spotted me, sweet rolls still securely in hand, collapsed on my knees on the Warsaw sidewalk.

After picking myself up, and still munching my delicious snack, we stopped to buy some towels. Although Sonia had said we were welcome to use the somewhat grubby ones in her vacant apartment, they appeared not to have been washed for quite a few months. We figured that unwashed but unused towels from *Universalniy Magazin*, the Universal Store, were likely more hygienic than unwashed and used ones from the apartment. I settled on two small, thin, scratchy, blue and white striped towels that served me well for my remaining year in Eastern Europe.

At bedtime a few problems arose. The bed, as I mentioned, was a twin. When Christine tried it out, the frame creaked ominously and the mattress sagged deeply in the middle. Surely it couldn't support the weight of both of us. We decided to take the mattress off the frame and lay it directly onto the floor. I was wearing a nightgown, and Christine toyed briefly with sleeping in the buff. She later decided to give in to modesty; her impromptu negligee consisted of a bra and a thong—I hope never to see a near three-hundred-pounder in that attire again.

We decided the most private sleeping arrangement would be to lie head to toe, so, with Christine on her two-thirds and me on my one-third of a twin mattress, we settled down to try to sleep.

A moment later Christine snarled, "You're touching me!"

Well, it was almost impossible not to have some unintentional contact given the girth of my companion and the miniscule size of the mattress. I was already clinging to the edge of the mattress as it was. This scenario was repeated two or three more times with me finally being catapulted onto the floor.

Christine decided it wouldn't do to have two of us in the single bed, and the only fair way to handle the situation would be for me to sleep on the cement slab kitchen floor and for her to have the bed. She, after all, was the one with the connections to her ex-boyfriend's mother, Sonia, in whose apartment we were currently ensconced. I succeeded in snatching from her hands a single blanket to provide me with a little warmth, cushioning, and comfort. To further support her argument, Christine let loose with a barrage of creative obscenities, followed by one final shove that propelled me from the living room into the kitchen. Then she slammed the door and locked it from her side, making my escape into a dark, cold, rainy, unfamiliar foreign city highly impractical, unlikely and downright terrifying. Personally, I think it would have been more equitable for the naturally padded one—Christine—to sleep on the concrete floor and the lightweight one—me—to have the bed, but in this situation, cowardice seemed the most prudent course.

At dawn, I tested the kitchen door and found it had been unlocked sometime in the night. Silently retrieving my belongings from the living room, I quickly dressed and packed my weekender, remembering to include my two new striped towels. I then began tiptoeing my way towards the front door of the apartment. Christine was in the living room, still asleep on the disassembled bed, snoring loudly. Unfortunately, my attempt at a surreptitious retreat proved unsuccessful.

From her soft mattress on the floor, she pleasantly asked me where I was going so early in the morning.

"I am returning to Moscow," I calmly responded in my best Chekhovian manner.

My colleague was seemingly oblivious as to why I chose not to join her for a leisurely breakfast and then later for a bit of shopping and sightseeing. Not wanting to discuss the matter further and risk another verbal assault, I bid her a hasty adieu and set off for parts unknown. Directionally challenged as usual, I began my trek to the train station, wherever that was.

Episode Nine

ABOARD THE POLONAISE

A gregarious middle-aged woman waiting in line behind me at the Polish National Railway office said "Hello" to me, first in Polish, then in Russian, next in German and finally in English.

After our short conversation of *"Sprechen Sie Deutsch?"* followed by *"Nein"*, we ruled out using German. As the line inched forward, the two of us randomly spoke the other three languages, as we punctuated each one with descriptive hand gestures and pantomime. Twenty-five minutes later, we had told one another an abbreviated version of our life stories and arrived at the ticket window. My new acquaintance graciously helped me secure a one-way ticket from Warsaw to Moscow. Then it was my *"Dasvidaniya"* to her *"Dawidzeniya"* ending with "Goodbye" and (a Polish-accented) "Goodbye".

The weather was brisk, I had a few hours before my train departed, and I was in the mood for a walk. Suitcase in tow, I followed the self-guided tour signs to Market Square at the center of Old Town, forty minutes away. I did quite well, really, arriving at my destination an hour and fifteen minutes later, having lost my way only a couple of times.

Old Town Warsaw, originally established in the thirteenth and fourteenth centuries, had been almost completely destroyed by the end of World War II, with all the Renaissance, Baroque and Neoclassical influence gone. But through the use of historical Italian landscape paintings, surviving architectural renderings, pre-War photographs and artwork, plus salvaged rubble, the city had been resurrected, literally brick by brick. So meticulous was its restoration that, in 1980, it was listed as a World Heritage site by UNESCO. Historic photographs showing the area before and after destruction, and then again after rebuilding, had been placed throughout the square, and these were stunningly poignant.

I returned to the train station, and, this time, having lost my way only once, completed the forty-minute walk in just under an hour. But once there, I was faced with finding the proper east-bound passenger train from a myriad of similar looking ones. All were waiting alongside one another on a multitude of parallel, converging, intersecting or diverging tracks. Not understanding written or spoken Polish, and with my abysmally poor sense of direction, I assumed that meeting up with this train was not going to be easy. I was right.

My train would remain in the station for only seven minutes after it had pulled in. Just ten minutes before its scheduled arrival, a loudspeaker announced in incomprehensible Polish and barely-understandable Russian that my conveyance would soon be boarding at Platform Six. I headed there and found my destination with surprisingly little trouble and with ample time to take a few deep breaths, calm down, get my bearings, and confirm yet again that I was in the right station at the right time at the right platform alongside the right set of tracks.

While I was taking one more deep breath, another loud rumble sounded from the public address system. As the announcement repeated, I understood that my train, the Polonaise, was due to arrive momentarily. But not at Platform Six where I was waiting. No, the Polonaise was currently on the tracks chug-chugging to its revised destination alongside Platform Eight. And, alas, in order to get to Platform Eight, I had to retrace my steps, with suitcase in hand, and climb three long flights of well-worn cement stairs, clunk-clunk my way across a reverberating metal bridge, descend three more long flights of well-worn stairs on the other side, wait for my train to pull in and stop, rush to my appointed car, hand over my ticket to the nattily dressed conductor, and climb on board. I managed to do this with eighty-seven seconds to spare!

I wheeled my forest-green Eddie Bauer weekender down the side corridor of the railcar, found my compartment, Number Five, and went in to stow my luggage under one of the three berths—a lower one as indicated on my ticket, thank goodness. Despite three decades of ballet lessons, I was no longer particularly graceful climbing up a narrow ladder into an upper bunk, assuming I was successful in getting farther than the second rung in the first place. And the close proximity of the ceiling wouldn't have helped my claustrophobia, nor would the often-stifling heat in the upper zones have helped my allergies.

Now I'd just have to wait and see who, if anyone, would be assigned to share my sleeper cabin. I was hopeful it would be one or two women. I wasn't eager to repeat a similar excursion on another overnight train when I shared a very small couchette with three very large and very intoxicated young men.

Surprisingly, I seemed to be alone, not only in my comfortable cabin, but in the entire train car as well. When we boarded in Warsaw, I was the only passenger to get on; that may explain why the stop lasted only seven minutes. And, when I entered the railcar, the doors to all the compartments, including mine, were open, with no one visible anywhere. An image of a dark blue hat trimmed in gold braid came to mind, but now the nattily dressed conductor who had worn that hat was nowhere to be found. Had I boarded the wrong train? Where were we going? When could I get off and reverse direction if I was now heading in the wrong one? And, just where *was* our conductor, anyway?

As the train snaked through town, I was enjoying the scenery from my very own large, freshly-squeegeed window. We had already left the historic parts of central Warsaw, had moved slowly through its unremarkable suburbs, and now the flat green countryside was before us. Suddenly the view changed to a drab, oppressive and heavily industrialized area. The Polonaise slowed to a leisurely stop.

Eight muscular men burst through the two end doors of my train car. With team-like precision they ran down the corridor, rolled up the narrow carpet and moved it aside. Then they threw open many of the windows, including the one in my compartment. They spoke a language completely incomprehensible and unrecognizable to me. I had no idea what was happening. Although certainly taken aback and puzzled, I didn't feel particularly threatened. Nonetheless, I huddled in a corner of my compartment, made myself as small as possible, and tried to keep out of everybody's way.

A petite woman in her mid-thirties, with dark braided hair, arrived with four of the brawny men in tow. The other four workers remained outside on the platform and passed bundle after bundle through open windows to their coworkers on the inside. Not only into my compartment, but into the neighboring ones as well. Resembling heavy, overstuffed pillows of varying sizes, these bundles were neatly wrapped in burlap and secured with twine.

In less than ten minutes, having transferred all the packages from outside to in, and then from adjoining cabins into mine, the inside team unrolled and straightened the carpet in the corridor just as it had been prior to the onslaught. They closed all the windows, ran off the train, and waved goodbye as my new compartment-mate, Alla, and I pulled out of the station on board the Polonaise.

Our three-berth compartment resembled the remains of a garage sale ransacked by hordes of bargainers. Alla apologized for the chaos and said she would have the jumble organized as quickly as possible. She immediately began tethering and strapping parcels onto her own upper bunk, as well as wedging them securely between the floor and each of the two lower bunks. She tested everything to make sure nothing would rattle or pull loose in the middle of the night. Since I would be sleeping directly underneath her bed, I was especially grateful for her thoroughness. So far there was no explanation as to what she was transporting in her burlap-covered bundles, or why all the male assistants had seen her off at the station.

We continued our slow passage through the outskirts of Warsaw and stopped briefly at another suburban station. A dark-haired, dark-eyed woman in her sixties boarded the train and took her place in our now fully occupied room. The woman introduced herself as Gohar. She was from Yerevan, and as an older Soviet Armenian, was fluent in Russian as well as her native Armenian. Other than Miss Hovsepian, my high school choral director, I had had very little contact with people of Gohar's ethnicity.

And I didn't know then, that upon my return to America in 1997, I would launch a career as a community college teacher of ESL (English as a Second Language). This would be in Glendale, a city in Southern California which is now home to the largest diaspora of Armenians in the world. By the time I retired in 2017, I had taught thousands of newly arrived adult Armenian immigrants ranging in age from seventeen to eighty-four. Some were altogether illiterate in their own language, and others had been astrophysicists, mechanical engineers, surgeons or language teachers. I taught a professional photographer, award winning film director, international chess master, architect, renowned fine artist, auto mechanic, auto designer, watchmaker, chef, former Olympic wrestler, and two or three members of the Armenian Mafia.

But I digress . . . Gohar, the Armenian in our train compartment had barely settled into her seat when she burst into tears. Between sobs, we learned that her purse had been stolen earlier in the day, along with all the purchases she had made in the open-air emporium in Warsaw. Gone were the two hand-knit sweaters for her son and daughter, woolen scarves for her sister, and felt slippers for her husband. Gone were the luminous amber broach and matching earrings for herself. Oh, and the intricately crocheted lace tablecloth for her upcoming party in Yerevan. Not to mention the sheep's-milk cheese, kolbasa, and local brown bread she had planned to eat during our journey back to Moscow. Gohar sobbed again, reflected that the thief had spared her life and that of the friend she had been visiting, and decided that things might not be so bad after all. At least she had retained her passport and a wad of money that was still hidden in a small silken bag beneath her blouse and jacket.

The other woman, Alla, the petite one who had the eight burly helpers, told us she was a "bobbin". And, as a bobbin, Alla spent about nine months of the year travelling between Warsaw, Moscow, Irkutsk, Ulan-Ude, Lake Baikal, Krasnoyarsk, Novosibirsk, and, finally, six thousand miles away, Vladivostok, at the far reaches of Siberia. Appropriately for a Russian port city on the Pacific Ocean, its name, Vladivostok, means literally Ruler (*vlad*) of the East (*vostok*).

The merchandise in Warsaw was far better than that in the old Soviet Union or the new Russia, and the prices were fair, Alla explained. She had purchased hundreds of items of clothing and accessories to resell at open markets in the above far-flung destinations, and was now transporting these bundled valuables inside our compartment as we headed to Moscow.

In Moscow, as in Warsaw, she would be met once again by another group of burly male helpers who would roll up the carpets, throw open the windows, and transfer all her precious cargo from the Polonaise onto another outward-bound train. This pattern would repeat itself in every major city along the way four times a year. On the non-stop return trip, there would be no need for strong helpers, as all the merchandise would have been sold, ideally at a good profit. Such was the professional life of an enterprising bobbin like Alla.

Every three months Alla returned home to war-torn Chechnya to her husband and their two children, but that meant another two-thousand plus miles on a train from Moscow to Grozny and back. Her husband, Ayub, remained in Grozny, rebuilding their home, which had been bombed out by the Russians for the second time in three years.

It was not Ayub, but Alla, who worked as the bobbin, because as a woman, and a tiny one at that, she would draw less attention from the authorities. Muscovite militia had an ongoing policy of roughing up and deporting suspicious individuals, and that included all darker-skinned men who were, or appeared to be, Chechen. Now, having left Warsaw less than an hour ago, Alla was just beginning her latest grueling trek. Without her entrepreneurial spirit, her family would be destitute.

It seemed Alla, Gohar, and I were going to be a highly diverse but very compatible trio. As customary, we ordered and paid for our sheets, pillows, and blankets from the conductor and settled in for our overnight journey to Moscow. The pleasant compartment had its own washbasin, lavender-scented soap, and bright white towels. A tiny porcelain vase, filled with blue and pink wildflowers, adorned a small oblong table anchored securely to our cabin's leather-padded metal wall. We shared some of the food and tea we had brought along. Russian was not the native language of any of us, but we managed to communicate well enough as we shared stories of our lives.

Several hours into the journey we stopped in Brest, at the border of Poland and Belarus (formerly Byelorussia) to go through customs. Local women boarded the train and sold us baked potatoes, bread, pierogi, and fruit for our supper, but if caught by customs they would likely be arrested. Although I had some Belarussian money, the only acceptable currency was American dollars or German Deutschmarks. The economy had completely collapsed in Belarus, making their money almost worthless. Even their own government agencies refused to accept Belarussian currency and required payment in US dollars.

One particularly animated Belarussian potato vendor spotted a customs official. Although selling her home-cooked fast food suppers enabled her to survive hard economic times, it was illegal for her to be on board our train. She quickly sat down next to me, hid her basket of potatoes under the seat, asked me to pretend that she was a friend and fellow traveler and to engage in a lively conversation.

I was a little reluctant to participate in this deception, but she was very persuasive, so we carried on with our friendly banter, she in her heavily accented and guttural Belarussian, and I in my equally heavily accented but softer sounding Russian. We talked about the weather, our families, dogs and cats, life's difficulties, and anything else that came to mind. After the customs officer departed, my jovial new acquaintance rewarded me with an extra baked potato flavored with garlic.

Before Alla, Gohar, and I settled into our bunks for the night, the conductor had told us that we would be going through customs again at 1:30 a.m. at the border between Belarus and Russia. Here our train would be elevated several feet off the ground for about two hours, in order to change the wheels and axles to accommodate a new gauge.

In Nineteenth Century Imperial Russia, designers of the Empire's new and rapidly expanding rail system chose a gauge for tracks that was a few inches wider than the track gauge in some, but not all neighboring countries. Expert opinions vary, but some say this plan was implemented to offer protection from invasion, or to at least slow down the invaders in their tracks, as it were. Hence, we could either get off the train and **stay** off for two hours during the changing of the mechanism, or remain on board.

While Gohar and I remained on board, customs demanded that Alla get off to account for all of her merchandise. In Alla's absence, Gohar confided that she generally disliked anyone who wasn't Russian or Armenian, and she thoroughly disliked Chechens. However, seeing how hard Alla had to work just to survive now prompted Gohar to have nothing but respect and empathy for her new friend.

When the wheels and axles had been changed and Alla was finally allowed to re-board, she was near tears. The customs officers had gouged her heavily for the privilege of bringing her goods into Russia, thereby eating up most of her profits. Not only that, but they wouldn't accept one of her one-hundred-dollar American bills, because it was a little wrinkled and bore a smudge on Benjamin Franklin's right cheek.

Russians were in the habit of taking only brand-new paper money, as they were fearful that used money might be counterfeit. Americans attempted to tell them that it was more likely that new, rather than well-used currency was counterfeit, but they would have none of it. I was able to exchange one of my new one-hundred-dollar bills for Alla's old one, and she was finally cleared through customs and allowed back on the train.

The three of us settled back into bed for the remainder of the journey to Moscow, arriving there the next morning. Gohar was met by her family, and Alla by a new contingent of burly men. We parted friends and I set out via the Moscow Metro on the short trip back to my apartment.

Episode Ten

A MITE-Y INVASION

Jerry, the amiable five-year-old black poodle, had no problems. My landlady Nadya and her thirteen-year-old daughter Katya had no problems. I, on the other hand, had problems in the form of a scarlet rash dotting my feet and shins. It looked relatively benign, but felt otherwise, as the rash was accompanied by intense itching. I tried lotions, creams, ointments, warm showers and cold soaks, applications of wet tea bags, and herbal potions made from dandelions or chamomile, gauze wraps and any other remedies suggested by meddling strangers or wise babushkas—nothing relieved the itching. And, the rash was slowly travelling up my legs en route to my knees.

It was summer, and the hotter the weather the more intense the itching. This was particularly true while I was riding any above-ground line on the Moscow Metro. Although the temperature in below-ground sections remained comfortable throughout the year, the above ground cars were freezing in the winter and stifling in the summer. The itching, though, was the worst of all while crisscrossing the city in a Khrushchev-era trolleybus. This might have been related to the several silver-dollar-sized, dust-spewing holes that had worn through the floor of the ancient conveyance. From these multiple openings, one could view the pavement in the summer, and the snow in the winter. This, in an era before ubiquitous handheld electronic devices, provided a mildly entertaining pastime.

I had been cautioned more than once never to touch any metal part of the trolleybus as long as one or more of my feet was in contact with the outside terrain. This was especially true in the presence of rain or snow. Apparently, the electrical system was not always adequately grounded, and each year a couple of wayward passengers would be zapped with a sometimes-deadly shock. Good luck, though, jumping twelve inches or more in and out of the trolley unassisted.

One day, after about three weeks of interminable itching, I finally spotted what I thought was the culprit—a miniscule varmint traversing my shin. I retrieved some scotch tape and adhered his little body to it. I counted his legs, and there were eight of them. Aha! The spider family. I did a bit of research in my *Merriam-Webster Collegiate Dictionary,* which had accompanied me from Los Angeles, and determined he must be a mite of some kind. So . . . Nadya and I set out for the most modern and technologically advanced medical clinic in Moscow, which, I should mention, hadn't been updated since the time of the Bolshevik Revolution.

We were the only ones in the waiting area, where we did, in fact, wait for a couple of hours. Finally, a jovial middle-aged doctor appeared wearing his tall white chef's hat—at least that's what the official Russian physician's headgear resembled at the time. I then presented this personable man of science with my tiny scotch-taped eight-legged specimen. The doctor agreed it was indeed a mite. Why I was the only one being eaten alive no one knew. Was there some special cream or miticide we could buy to solve the problem? Well, no, there wasn't. The only solution, the helpful doctor said, was to iron all the clothing, sheets and towels in our apartment. I knew that wasn't going to work—seriously, have you ever tried to iron a pair of shoes?

We returned to our apartment where Jerry the poodle greeted us enthusiastically. Nadya, just as enthusiastically, began stuffing newspaper wads into all the tiny crevices between floorboards and baseboards in our exceedingly (by Soviet standards) spacious three-room apartment. But, with parquet floors in every room, as well as in the hallway and kitchen, there were far too many nooks and crannies to make Nadya's stuffing enterprise feasible. Besides, since the mites were no bigger than a gnat's eyelash, all the paper wads in the world couldn't keep the critters from going about their business of biting me. I'd just have to suffer, but likely not in silence.

Nadya was at the bathroom sink scouring the newsprint off her hands when she shouted for me to come and look at something. A pair of well-worn blue jeans belonging to Katya were currently draped across the gleaming, streamlined, German-engineered Bosch washing machine adjacent to the sink. Nadya thought she had seen some tiny dark specks scurrying across the bright white enamel top of the washer. She now wanted me to confirm their presence. Hmmm . . . were they? Could they be? Well, maybe. Yes, yes, they were! A well-travelled band of enterprising mites had recently vacated Katya's jeans. They would likely be heading in my direction before nightfall. Word travels fast in the bug kingdom.

Katya, who had suffered no signs, symptoms or ill effects from the vagabond bugs, and who was still completely unaware of their presence, had been preparing to machine-wash her beloved blue jeans. This project, unprecedented as it was in the Stepanova household, required all of Katya's teen-challenged concentration. Not only was this to be a baptism of sorts for her Levi's, but it was also the first time she had used the washer, with the laundry chore always falling to her mother or her grandmother, Babushka.

The fact that my landlady Nadya actually owned a washing machine was nearly unprecedented as well, and it had been a major incentive for my deciding to rent a room from her. Everyone I knew said there were no laundromats in all of Moscow. Folklore had it that one (the only one) went out of business after two or three months as, it seems, the idea of such a convenience was just too novel.

As far as I could determine, Soviets had to wash everything—including bed linens—by hand in a bathtub or a sink, if they were lucky enough to have one or both of these receptacles. I was told that within the metropolitan area of large cities such as Moscow or St. Petersburg, indoor running water and plumbing were the norm. Not so for those on the outskirts, and certainly not for those in the countryside. Wouldn't want to think of trekking to a Siberian outhouse in the middle of winter! Well, summer wouldn't be so desirable either, considering that well-fed mosquitoes are said to approach the size of MIG47s.

For those destined to reside in a teeny one-hundred-or-so-square-foot communal flat, the kitchen as well as the bathroom/shower/toilet would have to be shared by five or six other households. In this case, by the way, each household generally had their own toilet seat and light bulb(s) which they carried with them whenever necessity dictated. One goal during the Khrushchev era was to provide every loyal Soviet citizen with at least one hundred square feet of space to call his or her own, a significant improvement, apparently, for the average person.

Throughout Moscow each summer, all the water was shut off for a few days, district by district, in order to check the delivery system. This was not particularly convenient. However, I have to confess that it was Nadya, and not I, who walked a few blocks to fetch three or four buckets of water from the tap of a friend who still had running water. Nadya returned the favor when the friend's water was shut off the following week.

And, as water was turned off in the summer, so steam was turned on in the winter. All of Moscow, I was told, was heated by steam which was sent throughout the city in huge (five or more feet in diameter,) above-ground pipes. Way above ground, and often over sidewalks, so that treacherous steep metal steps, resembling ladders more than stairs, had to be installed. Often these pedestrian crossings cropped up in the most inopportune spots—adjacent to a bus stop, next to a well-travelled walkway or at an exit from a large outdoor produce market. Here, I often saw babushkas hauling wheeled carts or carrying bags of seasonal fruits and vegetables up about fifteen metal steps, across a short, elevated walkway, and then down fifteen additional steps. All this, just to cross a sidewalk that spanned a mere six feet.

During my two years in Moscow (1995-1996), steam was provided for free, and, with a radiator in each room, was highly efficient in heating our apartment. The steam was turned on citywide after the recorded temperatures had plunged significantly below freezing for a requisite number of successive days. Once turned on, it could not be turned off in your abode until spring, when city officials had deemed the weather to be warm enough. Several times I visited apartments where the residents had sealed shut all the windows to keep out drafts, causing the interior temperature to approach tropical extremes. This was particularly unpleasant when dressed for an Arctic Moscow winter that was lurking just beyond the leather-padded, quadruple-locked front (and only) door.

However, I was especially lucky because my apartment building had little double-paned windows the size of small envelopes. Called *fortochka* (window leaves), they were nestled inside big double-paned windows, and could be opened independently of their larger counterparts. Opening the *fortochka* by themselves allowed a tiny breeze of sub-zero air to come in, and this was just enough to refresh the entire room. No need to crack open the larger windows and run the risk of flash-freezing any inhabitants or guests.

Such were some of the conveniences of Nadya's and my highly-desirable, three-room, thick-walled, well-built, Stalin-era apartment, a limited number of which had been registered many years earlier to high-ranking, elite Soviet scientists, including Nadya's parents and grandparents, and now to Nadya herself, an out-of-work professor of ichthyology.

One hot summer afternoon I came home after teaching my English conversation classes at the Japanese Embassy School. I was still under assault by the tiny mites that were nibbling on my lower extremities, and I was eager to take a cool shower to reduce the itching caused by the critters' bites. On the door of our first-floor apartment was a note from Nadya telling me not to come in, but to go directly to Babushka's apartment on the fourth floor. I was puzzled and a little bit worried, but did as instructed. Babushka was very noncommittal in her monosyllabic responses.

"Is Nadya OK?" I asked.

"*Da, da.* Yes, yes."

"Is the apartment OK?"

"*Da*, but it is necessary to wait."

"*Pochemy?* Why?" I enquired.

No answer.

"Where exactly is Nadya, anyway?" I wanted to know.

Still no answer. Babushka's friendly Persian cat, Masha, was somewhat more talkative, but nonetheless failed to divulge Nadya's whereabouts. Babushka prepared us some smoky tea and coma-inducing, sugar-infused cake slices, that is to say, a typically Russian dessert. She continued to remain friendly but mysterious and said that Nadya would phone us as soon as I was allowed to return home.

After a couple of hours, I decided I'd waited long enough and went downstairs. My very large, heavy, ornate key was useless, as the door was tightly fastened with several security bolts. After ringing the doorbell multiple times, I finally heard footsteps shuffling down the long hallway inside our apartment. From behind the door came a very muffled and distorted voice. In between exaggerated gasps and extended pauses, the voice told me in no uncertain terms to go away and stay away. In my most authoritative Russian, I demanded to know what was going on. The eerie voice ordered me to be quiet, go back upstairs to Babushka's apartment and continue to wait. I lingered outside our dwelling instead.

Forty-five minutes later the door opened, revealing a five-foot-tall creature with two very large bug eyes and a long, articulated trunk. Quite an unexpected sight for sure. Turns out it was Nadya sporting a vintage World War II gas mask. She had been busy all day fumigating the apartment and was hopeful that the fifty-year-old Red Army-issued apparatus might provide her with some protection against toxic chemicals. Soviet ingenuity had conquered the mite invasion.

Episode Eleven
INTERNATIONAL AID

It was ten o'clock on the first evening of fall semester, and I had just finished teaching my three back-to-back English classes at Moscow State University. My classroom was located on the eighth floor of an iconic, easily-recognizable, Stalin-era, multi-tiered, wedding-cake-inspired skyscraper that served also as dormitory and administrative offices. This was one of seven similarly ornate government structures, "The Seven Sisters", prominently scattered throughout Moscow.

I was heading to the nearby trolley stop, accompanied by two or three of my amiable postgraduate students. Rather than walking, I took the quickest and most direct route, falling down an entire flight of stairs and conveniently landing at my desired destination. My left shin had split open like a watermelon dropped from a vendor's cart. A Good Samaritan who was standing at the trolley stop, and who inexplicably had a first aid kit in his satchel, bound my leg tightly with gauze and said I'd be as good as new. I wasn't so sure. Treatment rendered, the impromptu medic wished me *"Nazdarovya!"* (good health), and boarded the trolley. While sprawled on the sidewalk, I attempted valiantly to maintain my image as a learned professor.

One of my students, Oleg, drove me home, engaging in polite conversation about our unseasonably balmy autumn weather, Moscow traffic jams, and the upcoming perils of winter driving. Well, it was more of a monologue on his part, actually, as I was gritting my teeth in pain and hoping not to faint. By Russian standards I seemed to have suffered nothing more than a minor gash and a bruised ego.

Upon entering my solidly-built Stalin-era building, I limped into the hallway of our first-floor apartment and was met by my landlady, Nadya, and Jerry the poodle. Dripping type-A-negative blood onto our parquet flooring, I hobbled down the corridor into the bathroom. There I perched on the edge of our blue-green tub and, in my best balletic form, extended my injured left leg alongside the adjacent wall, and planted my right foot outside the tub. Reminiscent of a sculpture by Degas, this dancer's pose allowed my blood to drip directly into the tub, rather than splatter onto the dingy black and white ceramic tiled floor. Closer inspection of my elevated left leg—first by Jerry the poodle and then by me—confirmed that I would need medical attention soon, but where and how?

Moscow didn't have any urgent care centers or walk in emergency rooms. Russian medical care, while inexpensive and universal, was also quite primitive. Equipment, including scalpels and scissors, was not properly sterilized, as there was no modern means to do so. Single-use intravenous tubing, catheters, and gloves were routinely used multiple times, as were disposable needles. Antibiotics, when available, had often passed their expiration dates. Not surprisingly, I hoped to find treatment in a facility where well-trained medical staff would use sterile instruments, and, as an added bonus, employ local anesthesia while suturing my wound. Meantime, the pricey ice-cold Smirnoff vodka I had been imbibing as a painkiller was working surprisingly well.

Nadya and I spent an hour on the phone trying to locate a clinic. Finally, we called Patricia, my British colleague at the Japanese Embassy School. Patricia had lived many years in Moscow, was married to a Muscovite, spoke fluent Russian, and knew her way around the city. Well, she told Nadya, she would forget seeking treatment in Moscow altogether; she would board the first plane back to England and make use of her British national health services. That's what she would do.

Unfortunately, that wasn't an option for me. Now out of the bathtub and back in my own room, I still had my leg elevated to slow the bleeding and save the flooring. I spent yet another hour on the phone, utilizing my best Russian, but to no avail. The Canadian Embassy Clinic wasn't answering its twenty-four-hour emergency phone. No help there. The French Clinic did answer their phone, but then I had to resort to my high school French to try to explain the situation. They would, however, be able to see me, but we would need to communicate in French. I said I'd get back to them. Finally, I called the International Medical Clinic and the phone was promptly answered by an Australian doctor. What a relief—someone who spoke English! Although he was currently at home and had been sleeping, Dr. Thompson agreed to meet me at the clinic at one o'clock in the morning.

The Metro had already closed for the day, but that was irrelevant as I couldn't walk well enough to get to a Metro stop anyway.

There were almost no official taxis in Moscow during the day, and there certainly weren't any to be hailed past midnight. After waiting quite a while on *Leninskiy Prospekt*, a major thoroughfare conveniently located not far from our apartment, Nadya and I finally flagged down a late-night driver who agreed to take us across town to the clinic for a reasonable fee. Amazingly, he was quite sober.

About thirty minutes later our intrepid cabbie dropped us off at a once elegant two-story neo-classical building with a crumbling mauve-colored façade. Perhaps once belonging to a successful nineteenth century Muscovite merchant, this previously opulent and privately-owned building had likely been confiscated by the Bolsheviks and subsequently collectivized by the Communists. We rang the bell several times before Dr. Thompson came to the door. He greeted us warmly in his cheery Aussie style and welcomed us into a sparsely furnished but altogether professional looking facility.

His assistant, Kostya Denisovich, who spoke limited English, beckoned me to the reception counter where he stood watch as I signed a liability waiver and an agreement to pay, in American cash only, for all services as soon as rendered. Anticipating this, I had brought with me all six of the crisp fifty-dollar bills that were previously hidden in the mammoth armoire in my bedroom. Kostya Denisovich counted out four, that is, two-hundred dollars, and placed the currency carefully into an envelope as collateral.

Legal and financial matters thus completed, my competent appearing middle-aged MD and his very youthful counterpart ushered me into a well-lighted and spotless examination room. Kostya, only twenty-four, was a qualified physician by Soviet standards. Not having been bogged down by extensive med-school academics or lengthy residencies and internships, he had already been practicing medicine, so to speak, for a few months. Recognizing that he might benefit from more training, Kostya had wisely availed himself of mentoring by the clinic's Western-schooled professionals. He was currently learning the duties of a medical assistant with the goal of ultimately practicing medicine at a more qualified level than previously.

Now it was his job to prepare my injured leg for suturing. He carefully applied a sterile solution, working from the distant periphery of the wound up to its bleeding edges, that is, from the unscathed outer areas towards the ragged inner margins. While wondering if I should mention to our trainee that he was in the process of breaking all rules of sterility, the experienced Aussie steered the neophyte *Russkiy* in the proper direction.

After anesthetizing the injured area of my leg, Dr. Thompson, with noteworthy theatricality, proudly and triumphantly opened his brand-new, securely packaged, gleaming, germfree, up-to-date surgical implements which, like the aforementioned local anesthesia, had arrived from the Land-Down-Under just twenty-four hours previously. It really was my lucky day, after all. Good thing, too, as the self-prescribed Smirnoff vodka was beginning to wear off.

With my leg now sutured, bandaged and compression wrapped, follow-up appointments having been scheduled, and discharge instructions reviewed, I limped out to the lobby to settle my financial obligations. Kostya, multi-skilled assistant that he was, had left the surgical suite moments earlier and was waiting behind the counter where, with the next-to-last fifty-dollar bill remaining in my wallet, I paid for my prescribed medications. Dr. Thompson reappeared and suggested I obtain a cane or crutch to help me with walking. That sounded like an excellent idea. As I had one lonely fifty-dollar bill lurking in my purse just waiting to be put to good use, I asked if I could rent or buy an ambulatory aid from the clinic. No, not possible, for although the International Clinic had ordered a large inventory of supplies, many of which had recently arrived, canes and crutches had been on back order for the past three months with no estimated delivery date on the horizon.

Not to worry, though, as Nadya resourcefully solved my need for a cane by mugging the babushka on the seventh floor of our apartment building. Well, actually, that's not quite what happened, but it makes for a good story, and, at any rate, I did gain temporary use of a cane. (In reality, the babushka, no longer mobile with or without a cane, was confined to her apartment where she was being cared for by her family.)

Because of significant bleeding into the joint, for several weeks I was altogether unable to bend my left leg at the knee. Consequently, while riding on the crowded Moscow Metro or any other mode of public transportation, my leg remained inconveniently outstretched. My fellow passengers didn't seem to object, however, and many of them decided my stiffened leg made an ideal shelf on which to rest their parcels.

On one occasion, still dependent on the borrowed cane, and laden with my school bookbag and a number of variously-sized packages of my own, I boarded a homeward-bound trolley. As there was no place to sit down, a gentleman in his eighties stood up to offer me his seat. I declined his kind offer and insisted that he remain seated. At this point another fellow traveler, a woman likewise in her eighties, spotted a nearby boy of about eleven who was comfortably seated alongside his mother. The eighty-year-old babushka stood up, glared at the boy and his mother, passionately lectured the pair about proper etiquette, commanded the adolescent to give up his seat to me, and to never, ever, anywhere, or under any circumstance, even remotely consider sitting down on another public conveyance until he was well into middle age. Whew and amen!

I, having already attained middle age some time ago, had now spent two full years in Russia, and they were joyous, melancholic, fascinating, and humbling. They were puzzling when, shortly after my arrival in January, I utilized roving snowdrifts as markers to find my way around Moscow; ludicrous when I made the mistake of travelling to Poland with my egocentric, super-sized-colleague festooned with nose rings, tattoos, and spiky, maroon-colored hair; highly amusing when besting Brian the Brit; frustrating, distressing and suspenseful when attempting (at the mercy of a minor bureaucrat) to renew my visa at the Russian embassy; magical while careening through the one-thousand-year-old village of Suzdal in a troika on a frosty Christmas morning; and humorous, captivating, mournful, mysterious, embarrassing, exhilarating, exhausting, and altogether glorious. Oh, and directionally challenging.

But, at last, alas, it was time to say goodbye to Mother Russia. *Dasvidaniya* and farewell.